nF419711

FLOWERING PLANTS IN THE PLAINS OF TAMILNADU

AQUATIC ANGIOSPERMS
Hydrophytes and Helophytes

FLOWERING PLANTS IN THE PLAINS OF TAMILNADU

AQUATIC ANGIOSPERMS
Hydrophytes and Helophytes

Dr. D. Subramanian

Professor of Botany (Retd.)
Annamalai University,
Annamalainagar – 608 002,
Tamil Nadu.

Chennai   Trichy   Tirunelveli   New Delhi

Honour Copyright
&
Exclude Piracy

This book is protected by copyright. Reproduction of any part in any form including photocopying shall not be done except with authorization from the publisher.

ISBN 9798223962823 **MJP Publishers**

All rights reserved   No. 44, Nallathambi Street,
Printed and bound in India   Triplicane, Chennai 600 005
MJP 770   © Publishers, 2024
Publisher : **C. Janarthanan**
Project Editor: **C. Ambica**

This book is Dedicated to

Sri Kanagambigai Amman

and

Lord Uchinathaswamy of Sivapuri,

near Chidambaram, Tamilnadu

PREFACE

In this book, Part III "Aquatic Angiosperms", the author has described the flowering plants living in water, rooted in the soil and leaves and flowers present above the water level, or totally submerged in water. The parts of the plants have been examined and drawn by the author, who has travelled almost throughout Tamil Nadu. As a teacher of over 30 years in Botany, Annamalai University, he has the experience of 25 years as Botanic Garden in-charge, in Annamalai University. Besides guiding Ph.D and M.Phil Scholars in Cytotaxonomy and Cytogenetics (30 Ph.D and 46 M.Phil), he has also published research papers in most of the families of flowering plants in cytotaxonomy, cytogenetics and chemotaxonomy in Advanced Journals. This book is the continuation of the previous book of the author on Flowering plants of Tamil Nadu, Part I & II Mangrove Flora and Marine Angiosperms.

More important plants, their uses, frequency of occurrence and the importance of taking conservation measures are provided in this book.

ACKNOWLEDGEMENTS

The author is thankful to **Dr.K.RANGASWAMY AYYANGAR,** his teacher in B.Sc., and M.Sc., Classes, guide in Ph.D Course and Professor and Head of the Department of Botany, **Dr.R.Ganesan, Dr.A.S.Lakshmanchary,** Professors and Heads of Dept. of Botany and **Dr.R.Sampathkumar**, Professor and Head of the Department of DDE, Botany, Annamalai University for having given valuable guidance, suggestions and useful informations about the flowering plants of Tamil Nadu.

He is also thankful to the authorities of Botanical Survey of India, Southern Circle at Coimbatore, Tamil Nadu for kindly permitting him to get the correct identifications of flowering plants, from the authentic records, for his cytotaxonomical studies.

The author expresses his sincere thanks to his Research Scholars particularly **Dr.R.Selvaraj, Dr.T.Govindarajan, Dr. N.Vijayakumar, Dr. L. Mullainathan, Dr. D. Thanavel, Dr. K. Ranganthan, Dr. Mrs.V. Kumutha, Dr. S. Mrs. L. Poongodi, Dr. Mrs.G. VijiStellabai, Dr. K. Annamalai, Dr. Mrs. A. Vimalavalli, Dr.M. Munian, Dr. N. Saravanakumar, Dr. A. Thangaraju, Dr. A. L. Chidambaram, Dr. K. Rajendran, and Dr. M.R. Kannan** for having collected very rare plants all over Tamil Nadu for their cytotaxonomical studies and also to all his friends who have helped him in multivarious ways in the completion of this book.

The author expresses his gratitude to the authorities of UGC, New Delhi for sanctioning the major research projects and the authorities of Annamalai University for sanctioning financial assistance for undertaking a large number of tours for plant collection with M.Sc. Students and Ph.D. and M.Phil Research scholars to various places of Tamil Nadu.

CONTENTS

INTRODUCTION

1. GENERAL INFORMATION

The author has classified the following plants of Tamil Nadu into six groups. The first group is Mangrove flora and the second group is Marine Angiosperms. The third group is the flowering plants living in water in the plains of Tamil Nadu. The fourth group is the flowering plants living in the soil of the plains from mean sea level to 1000 feet elevations. The fifth group is the flowering plants occurring in Eastern Ghats from 1000 to 4500 feet elevations like Kalrayan Hills, Pachamalai Hills, Shervarayan Hills, Kollimalai Hills, Thirunelveli Hills and Coimbatore Hills. The sixth group is the flowering plants present above 4500 feet upto 8500 feet elevations of Hill Stations, like Ooty, Kodaikanal and Valparai.

Gamble (1957) has enumerated flowering plants in 3 volumes, I, II and III from Tamil Nadu and neighboruing areas. Mathew (1990 to 2000) has described the flora of Tamilnadu, Karnatik with illustrations.

The present author is of the opinion that the plants of the plains are almost distinct from those of higher elevations of Hill stations like Ooty and Kodaikanal. Further, the aquatic plants are almost distinct from terrestrial plants in Tamil Nadu. Therefore, describing them all together is highly confusing and may not be clear to understand. Therefore, unlike the previous authors, the present author has classified them into six groups, based on their ecological situations.

Further the author has tried his best to distinguish the water loving plants into Hydrophytes and Helophytes. But, it is very difficult to achieve this because of the overlapping characters of the two categories in many instances.

Even though the author is trying to classify the different regions of plant collections like Mangroves, Marine Angiosperms, Terrestrial, Eastern Ghats and Western Ghats plants, some of the species of the plains of Tamil Nadu are also present in higher attitudes of Hill stations and the vice-versa. Some such plants are *Bixa orellana, Lantana camara, Dodonaea viscosa, Rhus mysorensis, Curculigo orchioides, Ageratum conyzoides, Centella asiatica, Acorus calamus* and some of the vegetable crops.

The author has described for the first time as new species from the plains of Tamil Nadu *Cleome prostrata, Habenaria triphylla, Aristalochia repanda, Crotalaria repens, Vigna Kanagambigai* and *Canna grandiflora* and published in Plant Archives and Indian Journal of Cytogenetics. The author has been growing these plants in his "Farm house" in his native place Ko-Athanur, Virudhachalam Taluk and herbarium specimens of them have been deposited at Botanical Survey of India, Coimbatore, Tamil Nadu.

Hydrocera triflora of Balsaminaceae has been found by the author some 20 years back in a small ditch at Poondiankuppam, Cuddalore District, Tamilnadu. The author has done cytological studies in this plant. The other genus Impatiens has nearly 80 species in Tamil Nadu but *Hydrocera* has 2 species worldwide. The rare species *H.triflora* has disappeared after the destruction of coconut garden in that place due to strong cyclone. Now, the author could not see that plant in those areas.

Another plant, a variety of water lily (*Nymphaea nouchali*) with small, sweet scented, bright blue coloured flowers called in Tamil "Neelothpalam" has been rarely observed by the author in small water ditches and canals in paddy fields on the way from Periapattu to Cuddalore bus route. But at present it is not found in these places.

The plain areas of Tamil Nadu, occupying most of the areas of this state will register + 100 to 108° F in hot summer. At this time most of the wild plants particularly annual herbs will disappear. The seed propagation is the only way for the survival of these plants. During rainy season, the seeds, wherever present will germinate and complete their life cycle before the onset of heavy summer.

More important species of flowering plants in the plains of Tamil nadu with illustrations by the author are described in this book. The diagrams are made from freshly collected specimens by the author.

Important plants have been made into herbarium specimens and sometimes preserved in 4% formalin and kept in author's home laboratory at 277, Mariappanagar, Annamalai Nagar – 608 002, Tamil Nadu.

2.   CYTOLOGICAL STUDIES

Cytological studies and Cytopolymorphism in Hydrophytes and Helophytes of the plains of Tamil Nadu.

Now-a-days, cytological studies are considered as a more important evidence to interpret the evolutionary trends and inter relationship among the taxa of any group of plants. Therefore, the works done on cytology by the author and his co-workers are included here.

Some of the species in the plains of Tamilnadu show variations leading to the formation of distinct populations. These populations are called morphotypes of a species, differing in a few characters among them. When these morphotypes are differing among themselves in sizes, morphology and number of chromosomes, they are called as distinct cytotypes or cytopolymorphs. These cytopolymorphs may be evolved as distinct varieties or even to distinct species in due course of evolution. A brief account of cytopolymorphs and somatic chromosome number of some species are described below:

S.No	Species	Present report of 2n number	Previous report author and year
I	**APIACEAE**	18*	18 Sharma, A.K.
1	*Centella asiatica* urban		and Ghosh 1954.
II	**ASTERACEAE**		
1	*Epaltes divaricata* cars	22*	
2	*Sphaeranthus indicus* Linn	20*	

*First report

3) Subramanian and Ponmudi (1987) have studied the cytological characters of some of the helophytic species of Scrophulariaceae.

III	**SCROPHULARIACEAE**		
1	*Stemodia viscosa* Roxb.	28	42, Raghavan and Srinivasan, 1940 b
2	*Limnophila heterophylla* Benth	34*	--
3	*Dopatrium lobelioides* Benth	14	14, Raghavan and Srinivasan, 1940b

4	*Moniera cuneifolia* Mich	80*	---
5	*Vandelia crustacea* Benth.	42	42, Raghavan and Srinivasan, 1940 b
6	*Ilysanthes tenuifolia* Urban	16*	--
7	*Ilysanthes oppositifolia* Urban	18*	--
8	*Scoparia dulcis* Linn.	40	20, Lewis et al. 1962
9	*Sopubia trifida* Ham	36*	--
10	*Micrargeria wightii* Benth	32*	--
11	*Angelonia grandiflora* Linn	20	20, Raghavan & Srinivasan, 1940 b
12	*Striga lutea* Lour.	40	40, Kumar & Abraham 1941
13	*S.densiflora* Benth.	40	40, Kumar and Abraham, 1941

*First record of 2n chromosome numbers in the respective species.

5) IV HYDROCHARIDACEAE

(B.Sivakumar, M.Phil thesis Guide Dr.D.Subramanian)

S.No	Species	2n Chromosome number	Chromosomal variations
1	*Hydrilla verticillata* Linn	22+2 sex chromosomes	2n=16, 24
2	Vallisneria spiralis	18+2 sex chromosomes	--

S.No	Species	2n Chromosome number	Chromosomal variations
3	*Blyxa aubertii* Rich	22	2n = 92, 24 and 16
4	*Ottelia alismoides* (Linn) Pers	22	2n=22,33,44,55,60,66, 68, 88, 110 and 132
5	*Nechamandra alternifolia* (Roxb.) Thwaites	14	2n=16 and 100

6) Cytopolymorphism in *Ottelia alismoides* (L) Pers (Subramanian D. 1991)

S.No	Species	2n Chromosome number
1	Plants, the largest of all the types studied, Leaves light brownish green and broadly cordate, Fruits broader and longer and winged.	2n=88
2	Plants slightly smaller than the above type, Leaves dark brownish green, Fruits slightly longer than broad and winged	2n=66
3	Plants smaller than previous one, leaves brownish green, and cordate; Fruits longer than broad, slightly winged	2n=44
4	Plants medium-sized, Leaves pale green and cordate, Fruit longer and narrower, without wings	2n=42
5	Plants large, Leaves light brownish green and broadly cordate, The fruit winged and broader below and narrower above	2n=22

S.No	Species	2n Chromosome number
6	Plants with small leaves light green and lanceolate with sheathing leaf base. Fruit narrow and long with small undulate wings	2n=68
7	Plants medium sized, leaves normal green and cordate. Fruit longer and slightly broader and slightly winged	2n=44
8	Plants very small, Leaves diffuse brownish green and lanceolate with sharp apex; Fruit slightly winged, and the smallest of all the types studied.	2n=44

The cytotypes 3, 7 and 8 have the same somatic chromosome number that is 2n=44 but they have distinct karyotypes (morphology) of chromosomes. The other cytotypes 1, 2, 4, 5, and 6 have both distinct karyotypes and chromosome numbers.

7) CYTOTYPES OF *URGINEA INDICA* (ROXB.) KUNTH (D.SUBRAMANIAN, 1978)

The author has recognized 9 cytotypes in Indian squill (*Urginea indica*) a helophyte of the plains of Tamil Nadu. Each plant is present as a colony (group) of 40 to 50 plants near by water resources. These groups are so distinct among themselves as to recognize them as separate varieties. They have distinct morphological and cytological characters. Therefore they are called cytotypes.

Cytotype   1=30+B Chromosomes

2=3n=30 chromosomes

3=2n=21 chromosomes

4=2n=14, 16 and 18 chromosomes

5=2n=20 chromosomes

6=2n=20 chromosomes but with distinct karyotype

7=2n=10, 12, 11 and 13 chromosomes

8=2n=20+B Chromosomes

9=2n=22 chromosomes

Each cytotype is distinct in morphological characters.

8) Cytotypes in *Crinum defixum*. ker (D.Subramanian, 1979)

The author has recognized 6 different types differing in morphological characters. These morphotypes have distinct chromosome numbers.

Cytotypes   1=2n=30 chromosomes,

2=2n=24 chromosomes,

3=2n=22 chromosomes

4=2n=20+B chromosomes

5=2n=20 chromosomes

6=2n=20+1, 2n=20 and 2n=19 chromosomes

The somatic chromosome number in all the species of *Crinum* including *C.defixum* and *C.latifolium* is 2n=22, only one cytotype (No.3) has 2n=22 chromosomes, the actual number for this species. All the other types show deviant chromosome numbers.

9) CYTOLOGICAL STUDIES IN CYPERACEAE. (D.SUBRAMANIAN, 1988)

In 18 species of Cyperaceae, cytological characters have been studied by the author. Of these, 2n chromosome numbers of some of the helophytic species of Cyperaceae are given below:

S.No	Species	2n number present report	Previous reports authors and years
1	*Cyperus triceps* (Rottb) Encl	22*	--
2	*Cyperus procerus* Rottb	18*	--
3	*Cyperus decumbens* Govindarajulu	18*	
4	*Cyperus exaltatus* Retz.	96*	
5	*Cyperus latovaginata* Govindarajulu	24*	
6	*Cyperus plumbeonucea* Govindarajulu	22*	
7	*Cyperus atternifolius* L.	32	32 Tenaka 1965
8	*Scirpus articulates* Linn	20	32 Sharma and Bal, 1956
9	*Eleocharis capitata* R.Br.	80*	
10	*Fimbristylis bisumbellata* Bub	16*	--
11	*Fimbristylis cymosa* ssp. *spathacea*	32*	

*First records of 2n chromosome numbers in the respective species

Excepting *Cyperus exaltatus* (2n=96) and *Eleocharis capitata* (2n=80), all the other species studied have lower chromosome numbers, whereas the terrestrial species of Cyperaceae, show higher chromosome numbers (Subramanian, 1988). Therefore, the terrestrial species try to become polyploids to withstand the unfavourable climatic conditions.

3. Ecological Adaptations

I. Hydrophytes

Pistia stratiotes is a free floating and the whole plant is soft with specific weight lesser than water, that is 1.0. The leaves are so organized like a boat moving on water surface. The plant body has soft parenchymatous cells. The leaves are coated with wax and so they will not be immersed inside water even though there is continuous raining for several hours.

In *Nymphoides cristata*, the stem resembles the petiole of leaves. But at the node of this stem, cluster of flowers and a leaf are produced. The stem is aerenchymatous with air cavities. The leaves resemble the lotus leaves, even though smaller in size with upper surface wax coating.

Therefore during heavy rainfall, the leaves will not be immersed. Similarly, the flowers are so arranged as to float on the surface of water.

The same mechanism is followed in lotus, *Nelumbo nucifera* and water lily, *Nymphaea* species. The modified stem is buried under the soil and the leaves and flowers are brought to the water surface by long petioles and pedicels. The rhizomes and seeds are medicinally important in lotus. The seeds have thick and stronger coats. Therefore, they will not be broken or destroyed by animals walking on the soil during summer.

The petioles are bulged like a balloon in the middle. In these, the bulged portion has air cavities in *Eichhornia crassipes* and help the plant to float on water. The whole plant is soft and light and the specific weight is less than that of water, that is 1.0. This mechanism helps the plant to float on water.

The air bladders in *Jussiaea repens*, 5 to 6 at a node of stem make the plant float on the surface of water. Then the plant will have more sunlight and aeration.

The leaves below the water level, immersed inside the water are highly dissected into hair like threads in *Lymnophila heterophylla*. But, the leaves above the level of water are broader and entire. The submerged thread like leaves are so adapted as to get more sunlight and aeration. The sunlight and aeration are lesser inside water than above the water level.

The more dissected hairy leaves of *Ceratophyllum immersum* and *Utricularia stelluris* is an adaptation to save the plants from fastly moving water during heavy raining.

Male and female plants are separate and present in one and the same place in *Vallisneria spiralis*. In both, the roots, rhizome and leaves are identical. Only in organization of sex organs, these plants are differing. In male plant, the flowers which are minute, simple and more in number are packed in a short pedicalled spadix at the base of the plants. At maturity, the spadix bursts open and the male sessile flowers rise up and float on the surface of water.

The female plant has long coiled soft cylindrical pedicel, longer than leaves, possessing at the tip elongated narrow cylindrical female flower. The petals are broader and help the flower to stand erect on the surface of water. Only the petals, ovary, style and stigma are on the surface of water. If water level increases, the coils of pedicle are relaxed and the flower is raised to the upper surface of water. If the water level decreases, the pedicel makes more coiling and brings the flower down to the reduced level of the water.

When the male flowers touch the female flowers, the anther bursts open and the pollens touch the stigma and pollination is effected. This is a typical example of water pollination mechanisms, the hydrophily.

Besides, the leaves are narrow, thin and thick green like a green ribbon, present inside the water. The leaves are so flexible as to avoid breakage during strong water waves at the time of heavy rainfall and flood.

Blyxa aubertii is another hydrophyte in Tamilnadu plains. They have thin, soft light green sword like leaves produced from the underground tuber. Here also the leaves are very thin so that they may not be broken into pieces during heavy water current. This plant is present in pure water sandy soil and the light green leaves can easily absorb sunlight. The plants are present in less than 1 foot depth of water. The leaves have no midvein and the leaves are separated into many rectangular compartments. The whole leaf is transparent and shines like golden particles under sunlight. It is the most beautiful and attractive of all the hydrophytes.

In ***Potamogeton pectinatus*** there is no difference between stem and leaves. They are cylindrical and needle like. The heavy floods cannot break the parts of this plant even though they are present completely submerged under water. Then and there, small flower clusters are present in the nodes of stem and they will not be disturbed due to fast flowing water.

Potamogeton nodosus has tongue shaped leaves and it is common in small ditches to large water reservoirs. But *P. pectinatus* is very rare and present in large lakes and water canals in fastly flowing water. Therefore, this species has needle like leaves and stems.

Hydrilla verticillata, Elodea sp, and **Nechamandra alternifolia** have smaller, narrower and flexible blades of leaves to escape from ecological disturbances as they are totally submerged inside water.

During summer, we can collect large number of lotus seeds, brownish black and oval in shape in the lakes where there have been lotus plants. The seeds have thick and strong seed coats. When the animals walk on the lake, these seeds will not be so easily broken. In the next rainy season they germinate. The rhizomes of this plant are eaten by animals and human beings.

2.   HELOPHYTES

Like date palm trees (*Phoenix sylvestris*) present on the borders of small water ditches very rarely in large deserts of the world like sahara, etc., the helophytic plants can be seen in colonies on the banks of rivers, water canals, ditches, lakes, ponds, etc. These plants are not seen in terrestrial habitats. They are not also living as hydrophytes inside the water forever.

But, extensive field trips are necessary to find out and describe some more helophytes from Tamil Nadu. But, it is not easy to add a particular plant under helophytes in some of the cases.

The helophytic plants have some special adaptations like stilt roots as in *Pandanus*; two types of leaves (heterophylly) one under water (dissected and narrow leaves) and the other above the water level (broad and entire leaves for photosynthesis, etc.) as in *Limnophila heterophylla*. Air bladders in the axils of floating stem on water like *Ludwigia adscendens* (*Jussiaea repens. L*) are spongy and soft with more air spaces to make them float on water surfaces like *Aeschynomene* species, *A. aspera* L. and *A. indica* and *Ipomea aquatica* Forsk (hollow stem). Leafless stem with dark green colour and central large cavity are present in *Cyperus articulates* L., *Eleocharis acutangula* (Roxb) Schultes and *E. spiralis* Roemer & Schultes, *E. dulcis* Hansche and stem like petioles having cluster of leaves and inflorescences at the tips like most of the Cyperaceae members (*Cyperus rotundus, C. tenuispica* Steudel, *Schoenoptectus articulatus* (L) Palla; *S. juncoides* Palla, *S. lateriflorus* Rye, *S. litoralis* Palla. and *S. mucronatus* Palla.

In *Centella asiatica* the stem is cylindrical, soft and creeping. At each node, cluster of roots are produced below the soil and cluster of short petioled leaves above the soil. Even if the branches are cut off, each node with roots and leaves will establish itself as a new plant.

The bulbous plants, *Urginea indica, Crinum defixum* and *C. latifolium* have large underground bulbs. During summer, the leaves and inflorescences dry up and the bulbs are protected from hot climatic conditions as they are buried under the soil as colonies (20 to 30 bulbs in a cluster in *U. indica* and 4 to 5 bulbs in the species of *Crinum*). *Saccharum spontaneum* has thick underground rhizome along with aerial erect stem with leaves and inflorescences. During heavy summer, the aerial parts dry up but the underground rhizomes will be alive undergoing a condition of dormancy. During the next favourable rainy season starting, the aerial stems start growing with leaves and inflorescences. Similar is the case in *Colocasia antiquorum* in which the underground bulbs act as perennating organs.

Likewise, in wild paddy *Oryza meyeriana* and *O. glabrescens*, the fruits on maturity fall down and get buried inside the mud of 1 to 2 feet depth. In the next rainy season, they start germinating with soil having thin film of water and establish in the same place as usual. Nobody is collecting the seeds, preserving them during summer and sowing in the next rainy season. But these wild paddy have been found in the same place for several years during the rainy seasons alone. This is true in most of the seed producing plants living in wet and marshy places of the plains of Tamilnadu, particularly Cyperaceae and Poaceae members.

In *Colocasia antiquorum, Typha angustifolia, Acorus calamus, Crinum defixum, C. latifolium, Urginea indica, Canna generalis, C. grandiflora* and *Calamus rotung,* seedlings are produced by the side of the mother plant, a means of vegetative propagation. Seed germination and multiplication of progenies are very rare in these plants. But, Cyperaceae, Gramineae, Scrophulariaceae, Polygonaceae, Acanthaceae and Gentianaceae members multiply their progenies only by seeds. *Ipomea carnea* is a large shrub with pink, large tubular flowers established recently in the plains of Tamilnadu. It has semierect branches. It is always as colonies on the borders of water canals, ditches and wastelands and marshy substratum. It is called in Tamil "Neyveli Kattamani". In some cases, the flowers are so brightly coloured and showy as to be cultivated ornamentally.

PART III

AQUATIC ANGIOSPERMS OF PLAINS OF TAMIL NADU

1. HYDROPHYTES

These plants adapt themselves to live inside the fresh and undisturbed water sources or free floating or rooting inside the soil and the aerial parts floating on water surfaces of ponds, ditches, lakes, water canals, small rivers, etc. These hydrophytes come under the families, Nymphaeaceae, Alismaceae, Pontederiaceae, Hydrocharitaceae, Potamogetonaceae and Najadaceae. Very rarely, the species of other families live as Hydrophytes like *Pistia stratiotes* of Araceae, *Nymphoides cristata* of Menianthaceae and some members of Cyperaceae and Poaceae.

FAMILY 1: NYMPHAEACEAE

The species are aquatic perennial herbs. Gamble (1957) has recorded two species of *Nymphaea* and one species of *Nelumbium* in the plains of Tamilnadu.

1. *Nymphaea Stellata Willd* (Plate - 1)

The leaves are entire or sinuate, glabrous on both sides, produced from underground rhizome. Flowers are blue, white, rose or purple and the plants are available in small tanks, ditches and water canals. The blue flowering varieties called "Neelorpatham" are very rare (Plate - 4). It is having scented flowers and is fast disappearing from earth due to human disturbances. The author has seen the plants from Alappakkam to Cuddalore in small water ditches or canals by the side of paddy fields. This variety is almost different from other varieties of *N. stellata*.

2. *Nymphaea Nouchali Burm* f. (N.pubescens Willd.) (Plate - 2)

This species is very common with white or red flowers, found in all districts of Tamilnadu. The flowers of this species are larger than those of the previous species.

Apart from these two species, there is an ornamental variety with red or purple large showy flowers grown in small cement circular pots with mud at the bottom and water above. This plant is almost distinct in leaf and flower characters when compared to the above two species. **(Plate - 3)**

Recently from 2016 onwards, in the shallow water of uncultivated lands by the side of Muthiah Medical College and Hospital, a large number of small plants with small white flowers **(Plate - 5)** have been observed. It is mostly different from other varieties and species of *Nymphaea* already present throughout Tamil Nadu. These newly occurring variety can be living in ½ feet depth of water. The author has seen this variety in Virudhachalam and Chidambaram area of Cuddalore District then and there, rarely. Further studies are in progress in this variety.

3) *Nelumbo Nucifera* Gaertner (*Nelumbium Speciosum* Willd.) (Plate - 6)

This is commonly called "Lotus" plant. There are two varieties, pink and white flowering. In a particular lake in Tamilnadu it is observed that any one of these two varieties may be present, but not both.

The flowers are valued as sacred flowers for worshiping God, for preparing garlands and also for curing some diseases of human beings. The seeds are edible. Sometimes, the rhizomes are cooked and eaten by village people. The leaves are used like banana leaves for taking food. In full flowering, the lake is very beautiful and attractive.

FAMILY 2: MENIANTHACEAE

Once *Nymphoides cristatum* (Roxb.) Kuntz (Plate-7 (*Limnanthemum cristatum* (Roxb.) Goriseb) was put under the family Gentianaceae but recently it was separated from it and put under a separate family Menianthaceae. This plant is a free floating aquatic herb resembling a miniature lotus plant and occurring in still waters of small canals or water ditches. The stem is runner like resembling petioles of leaves. From this stem a cluster of flowers appear. The flowers are like those of Gentianaceae members, small, below 1 cm diameter and white.

This species is fast disappearing due to heavy floods, continuous drought, human disturbances and invasion and fast spreading of *Ottelia alismoides* covering almost all the surfaces of canals and lakes and leaving no space for the presence of *Nymphoides cristatum.* Therefore we have to preserve this plant by taking suitable conservation methods.

FAMILY 3: LENTIBULARIACEAE

Utricularia stellaris L. f **(Plate - 10)** is present in sandy soil with fresh and pure water during rainy seasons. It is having a large number of bladders among the leaves to catch insects. So, it is called bladder wort. It is completely immersed inside water. The author has collected it at sand dunes of Puduchattiram and many places of Cuddalore District.

FAMILY 4: ARACEAE

1. In this family, there is a small free floating aquatic herb, *Pistia stratiotes*, L. **(Plate - 8).** The stem is stoloniferous producing cluster of roots below and leaves above at each node. Sometimes, spadix inflorescences arise from the nodes. Even though small, it is very beautiful. Already a variety with larger leaves is rarely grown as ornamental plant in nursery gardens.

2. *Cryptocoryne retrospiralis* (Roxb.) Kunth **(Plate - 8)**. It may be considered as both hydrophye and helophyte but it never grows in mesophytic wet soils. It is a peculiar plant with erect underground rhizome buried inside the loose clay soil on the borders or inside water canals. The leaves arise above the soil and submerged almost or partly inside water. But the spadix and fruit clusters have been completely buried inside the loose clay soil. Therefore, throughout the year we cannot see the inflorescences or fruit clusters in this plant on the surface. After maturity, the fruits burst open and seeds are liberated inside the mud. In the next favourable season,

these seeds germinate and so always clusters of plants make dense colonies in a particular place, more crowded together. In 1972, the author, as a research scholar in the Department of Botany, Annamalai University, wanted to get these plants with rhizomes and so removed the clay and took a few mature plants. These plants had inflorescence and fruit clusters. The inflorescence was spirally twisted and after thoroughly washing, we could see the flowers. Only 0.2 or 0.3 cm tip of inflorescence was above the soil and in the cluster of crowded plants, it was too small to see it. Then my Professor and Head and my Guide Dr.K.Rangasamy Ayyangar identified it as *Cryptocoryne restrospiralis*.

FAMILY 5: CERATOPHYLLACEAE

Ceratophyllum demersum. L **(Plate - 9)** is the only plant of this family.

It is a slender, common submerged water herb looking like an alga, 1 to 3 feet long. Leaves are whorled, dichotomously branched into filiform, minutely toothed lobes without stipules. Flowers are minute, monoecious, solitary, axillary and sessile.

FAMILY 6: HYDROCHARITACEAE

This is a larger family of aquatic angiosperms having more number of species in the fresh waters of the plains of Tamil Nadu.

1. *Hydrilla Verticillata* (Linn. F.) Royle.

It is a slender submerged herb. The leaves are 3 to 4 whorled at a node, entire or toothed, linear-lanceolate with clear midrib. Flowers are monoecious or dioecious. Inside water these plants form dense and dark green mats. They are found inside still waters of ditches, water pits, rice fields and small water canals.

2. *Vallisneria Spiralis* Linn (Plate - 13).

It is a submerged tufted stemless stoloniferous fresh water herb. Leaves are long, linear, flat and flexible.

Minute male flowers are present in a shortly peduncled ovoid 3 lobed spathe present only in male plant. Solitary female flowers are present in tubular 3 toothed spathe one in each spathe at the end of a very long filiform spirally coiled scape in the female plant. When the water level increases, the female flowers rise up to the level of increasing water surface by relaxing the coiled scape. After released, the male flowers float on the surface of water. When the male flower touches the female flower, the pollen grains of male flower touches stigma of female flower and pollination takes place. It is a typical example of hydrophily.

3. *Blyxa Octandra* (Roxb) Planchan ex. Thwaites (Plate - 14) (*B. Roxburghii* Rich.)

It is a dioecious submerged stoloniferous, tufted, scabigerous herb. Male and female flowers are present in the same plant. Male spathe is pedicilled and female spathe is sessile. The leaves are broad below and reduced in breath towards the tips. They are sword like. The leaves are shining and transparent, yellowish green and very beautiful to look at inside the fresh water. The author has collected this plant in sandy soil paddy fields with pure still water near Kannankulam of Sirkali Taluk.

4) *Ottelia Alismoides* Pers (Plate - 15)

It is a succulent flaccid herb with fibrous roots. Leaves are submerged, very variable, oblong or orbicular, cordate, membranous, undulate, 7-11 nerved, petiole trigonous. Flowers are solitary, monoecious sessile within a tubular long pedunculate spathe. Spathe is 5 to 6 winged, undulate and unequal; Fruits ellipsoid crowned by the withered perianth. Commonly present in lakes, tanks, ditches and water canals.

5) *Nechamandra Alternifolia* (Roxb.) Thwaites (*Lagerosiphon Roxburghii* (Planchan). Benth.)

This is a submerged fresh water herb. Leaves are alternate or sometimes crowded and subverticillate and the lower leaves opposite, serrulate or entire shallow lanceolate. Flowers dioecious, male and female plants separate. Male flowers are minute, numerous in an axillary, sessile, ovoid 2-fid spathe, Female flower is solitary sessile in a narrow oblong spathe. It is commonly present in tanks of all districts of Tamil Nadu.

FAMILY 7: PONTEDERIACEAE

1. *Monochoria Vaginalis* Presl.

It is present in all districts of Tamil Nadu in the plains up to 3000 feet elevations. It is a fresh water and marsh herb, rooted in mud and erect or floating if submerged. Flowers bisexual irregular in spikes arising from the sheath of the upper most leaf, blue usually spotted with red. Leaves are ovate or subreniform base rounded or cordate, petiole upto 20 inches long. It is usually present in the borders of perennial water canals and ditches, etc.

2. *Eichhornia Crassipes,* Solms (Plate - 16)

It is an introduced American plant found in water canals and lakes in rainy season. In summer it is rooted in the wet soil but during winter it is free floating. Even though it is wild, the peculiar swelling of petioles and colourful flowers in clusters are very beautiful. The swollen petioles are helping the plants to float on water surfaces. The plants are so much crowded as to prevent the water flow and the growth of other plants like waterfily, lotus, etc.

FAMILY 8: ALISMACEAE

1. *Lymnophyton Obtusifolium Miq.* (Plate - 11)

Plants 3 to 4 feet high, leaves reniform, or deltoid sagitate, apex rounded or sometimes acute. Panicle infloresences are upto 3 to 4 feet in height with clusters of white flowers intermittently. It is a beautiful plant present in small water pits, ditches and water canals. This is a rare plant available in Tamil nadu but due to human disturbances and continuous drought for one or two years, these plants are fast disappearing.

FAMILY 9: APANOGETONACEAE

1. *Apanogeton Natans* Engl. (Plate - 17)

Inside stagnant water near paddy fields and ditches and borders of water canals, the plant is rooted in the soil but leaves are above water levels. The white pink or pale blue flowers in clusters are seen at the tip of the plants, 1 to 1½ foot in height. It is common throughout Tamil Nadu in rainy seasons. Gamble (1957) and

Mathew (1991) have recorded two species of *Apanogeton* but the other species *A. echinatus* is very rare.

FAMILY 10: POTAMOGETONACEAE

Submerged or floating plants in large tanks, lakes, stagnant water sources, etc. Gamble (1957) has recorded 5 genera under this family; namely *Potamogeton, Ruppia, Zenichellia, Cymodocea* and *Diplanthera*. Of these *Potamogeton* is a common fresh water plant. *Potamogeton* has 4 species in Tamil Nadu. Of these, two species *P. nodosus* and *P. pectinatus* are common.

1. *Potamogeton Nodosus (P. indicus. Roxb.)* (Plate - 17)

This plant is present in all the districts of Tamil Nadu. Upper or all the leaves are floating. They are broad and petioled. Stem is terete and branched. Peduncles are axillary or leaf opposed. Spikes are dense flowered.

2. *Potamogeton Pectinatus* Linn

This plant is rare, stem is filiform and many branched, leaves are narrowly linear or filiform. There is no difference between stem and leaf. Sometimes, it is present along with previous species. The author has collected this plant during summer, when the water is scarce at Veeranam tank some 10 years back.

FAMILY 11: NAJADACEAE

Gamble (1957) has recorded 5 species and 2 varieties under the single genus *Najus*. The author has seen long back a species of this genus in a water canal in his native palce, Ko-Athanur, Cuddalore

District. It is a freshwater submerged plant, 1 to 1½ foot long and at each node 3 to 4 linear spiny leaves are present and so it is spiny in texture. In 2000, the author has collected *N. minor var spinosa* at Mandapam near Pamban bridge. The leaves and stem are spinous all over the plant.

FAMILY 12: LEMNACEAE

There are two genera *Lemna* and *Wolffia* present in Tamil Nadu under this family. They are floating aquatic minute plants with globose or subglobose leaves, *Lemna* has two species *L. paucicostata* Hegelin and *L. parhiva* Linn and *Wolffia* has one species namely in Tamilnadu.

EXPLANATION OF PLATES AND FIGURES

HYDROPHYTES

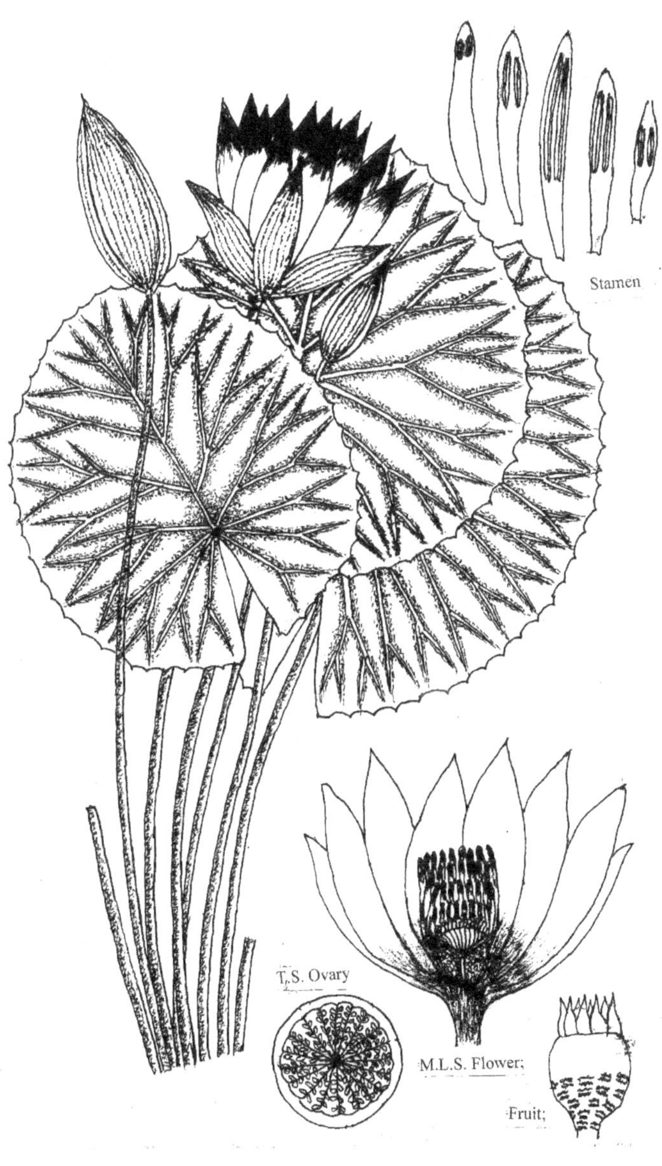

Plate 1   *Nymphaea stellata*

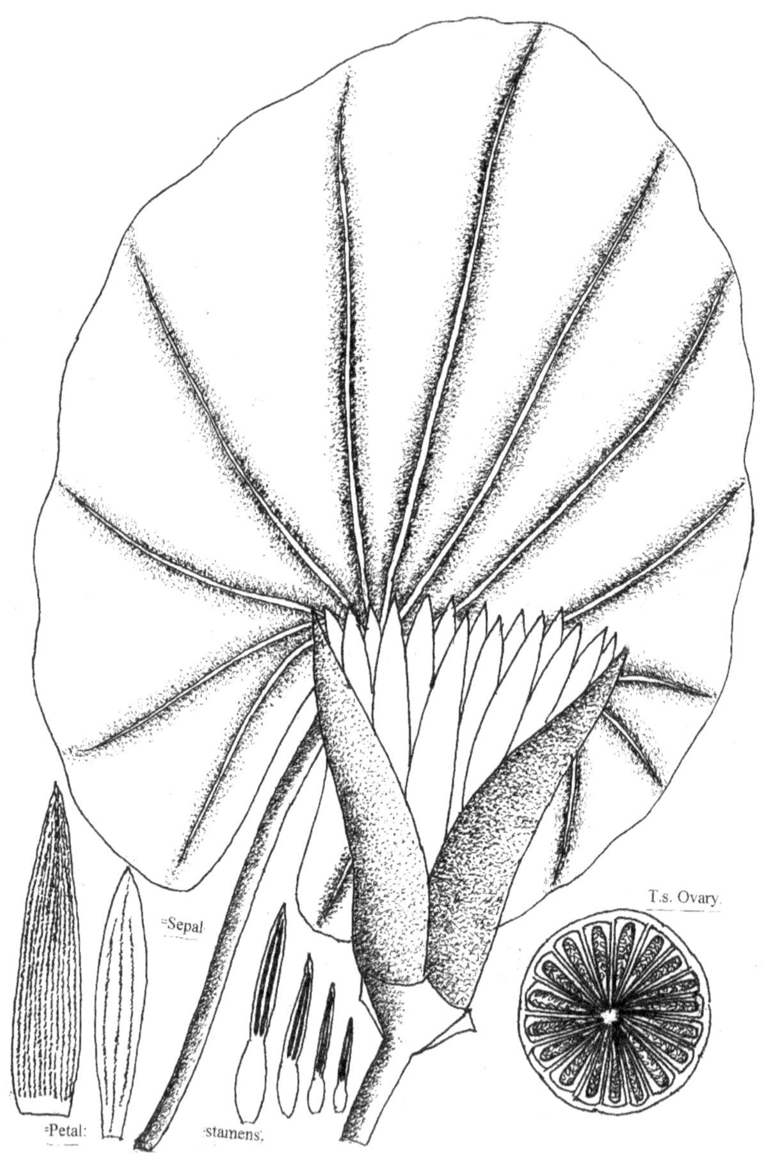

Plate 2 *N. nouchali*

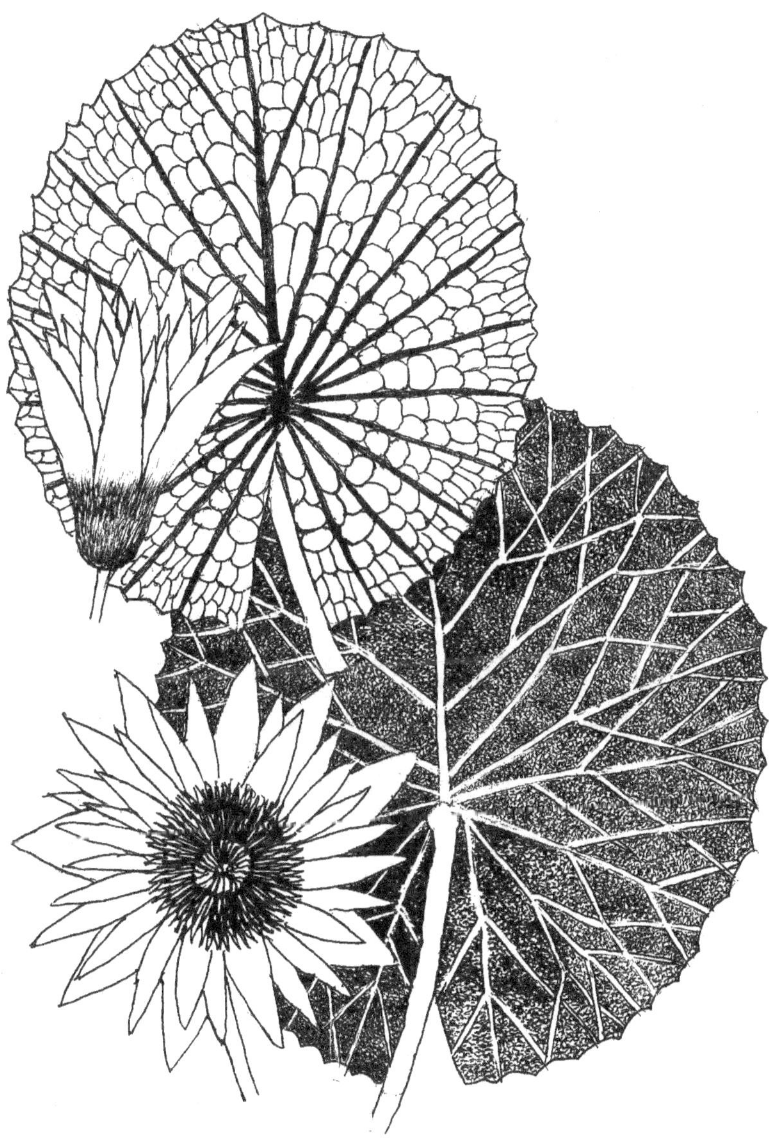

Plate 3 *Nymphaea* cultivated variety

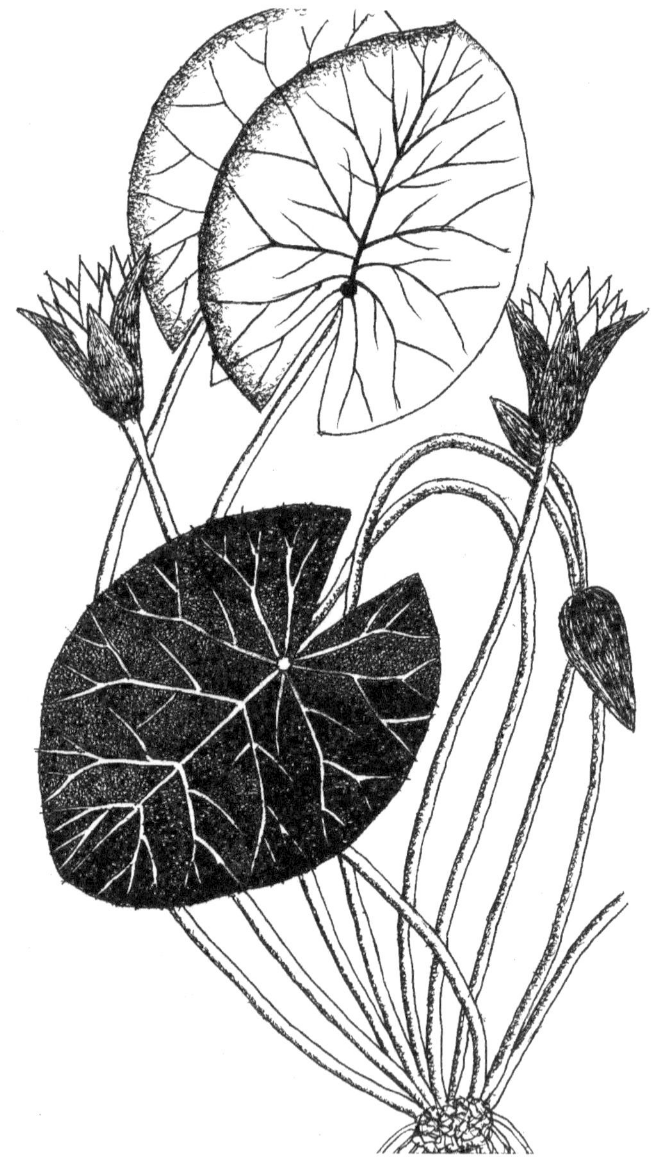

Plate 4 *Nymphaea* wild blue flowering variety.

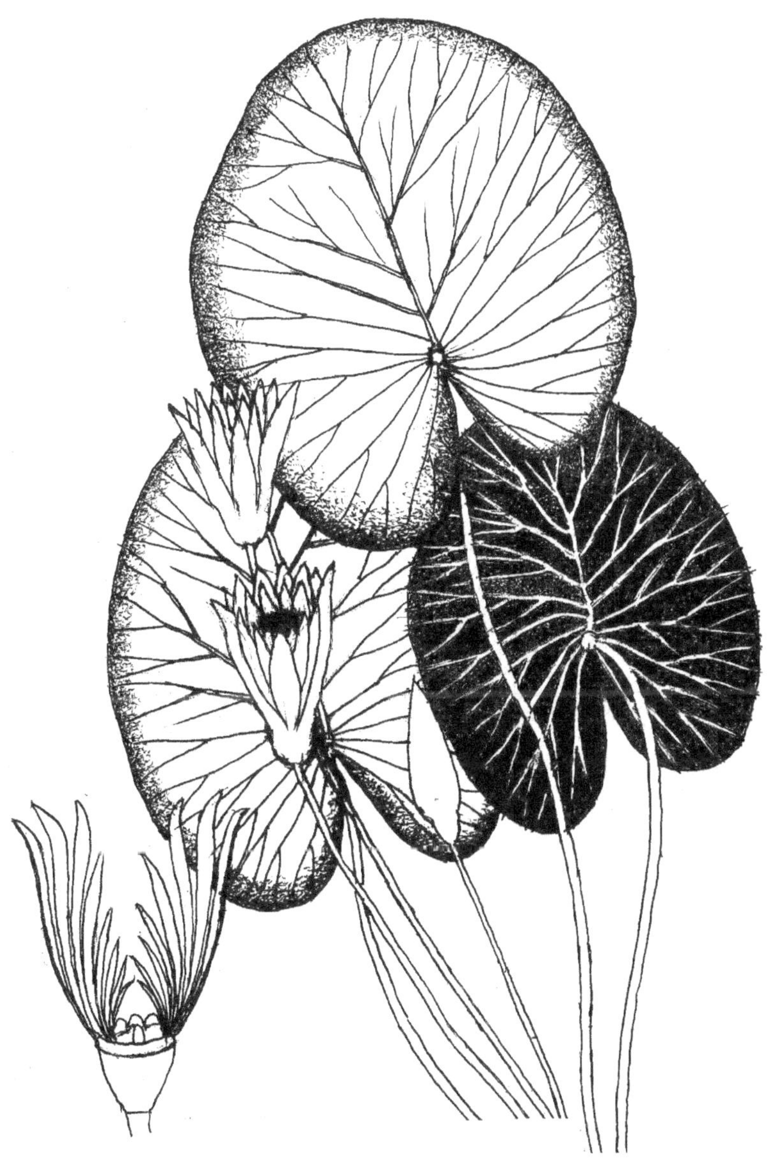

Plate 5 *Nymphaea* **wild white flowering variety**

Plate 6   *Nelumbo nucifera*

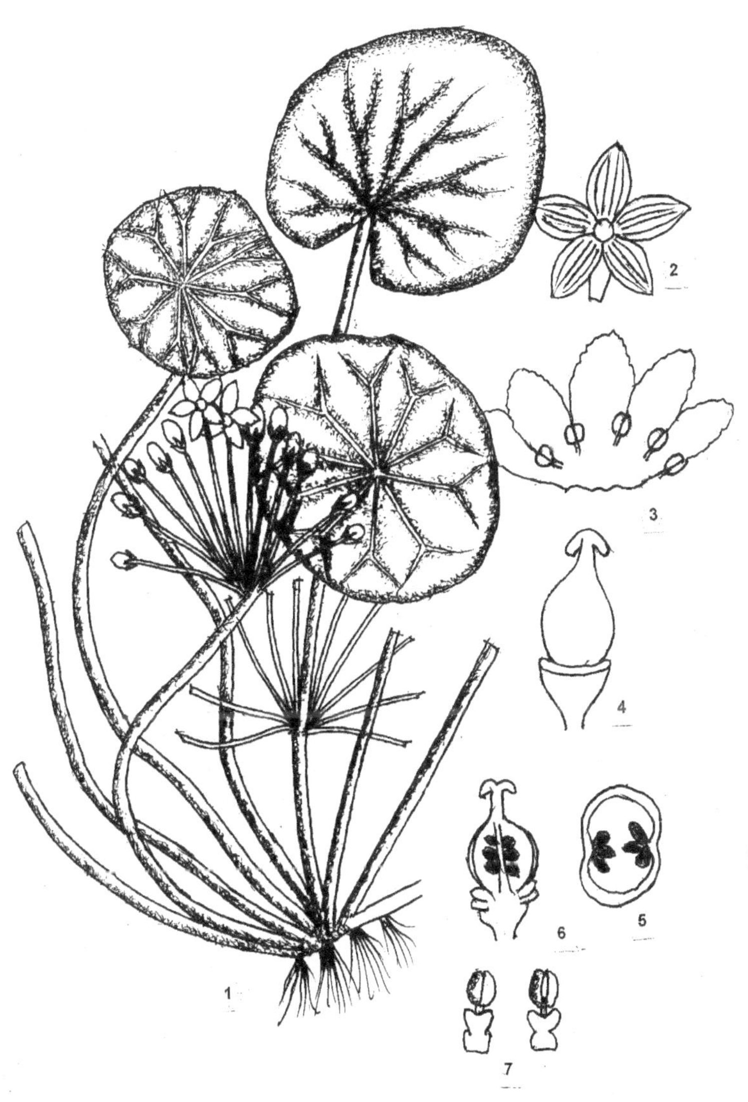

Plate 7   *Nymphoides cristata;* **Figure** 1 = A plant; 2 = Flower; 3 = Petals with stamens; 4 = Carpel; 5 and 6 = L.S. and T.S. Ovary; 7 = Stamens.

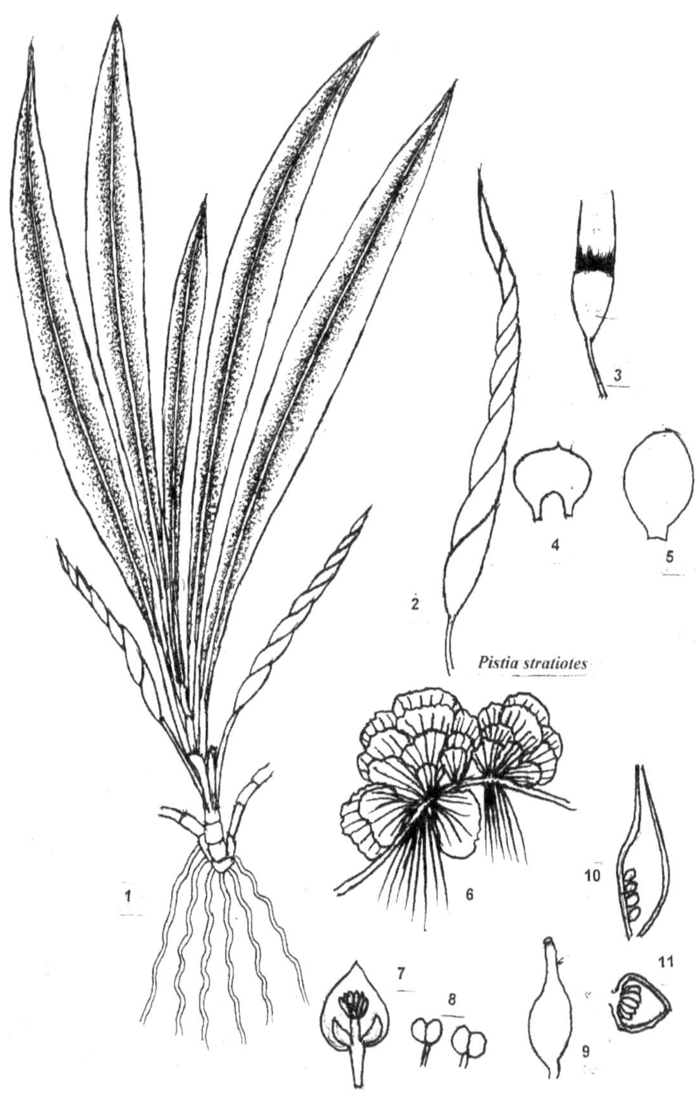

Plate 8   *Cryptocoryne retrospiralis;* **Figure** 1 = A plant; 2 = spadix; 3 = part of spadix; 4 = Stamen; 5 = Carpel. **Figure** 6 to 11 = ***Pistia stratiotes;*** **Figure** 6 = Habit; 7 = spadix; 8 = stamens; 9 = carpel; 10 and 11 = L.S. and T.S.ovary.

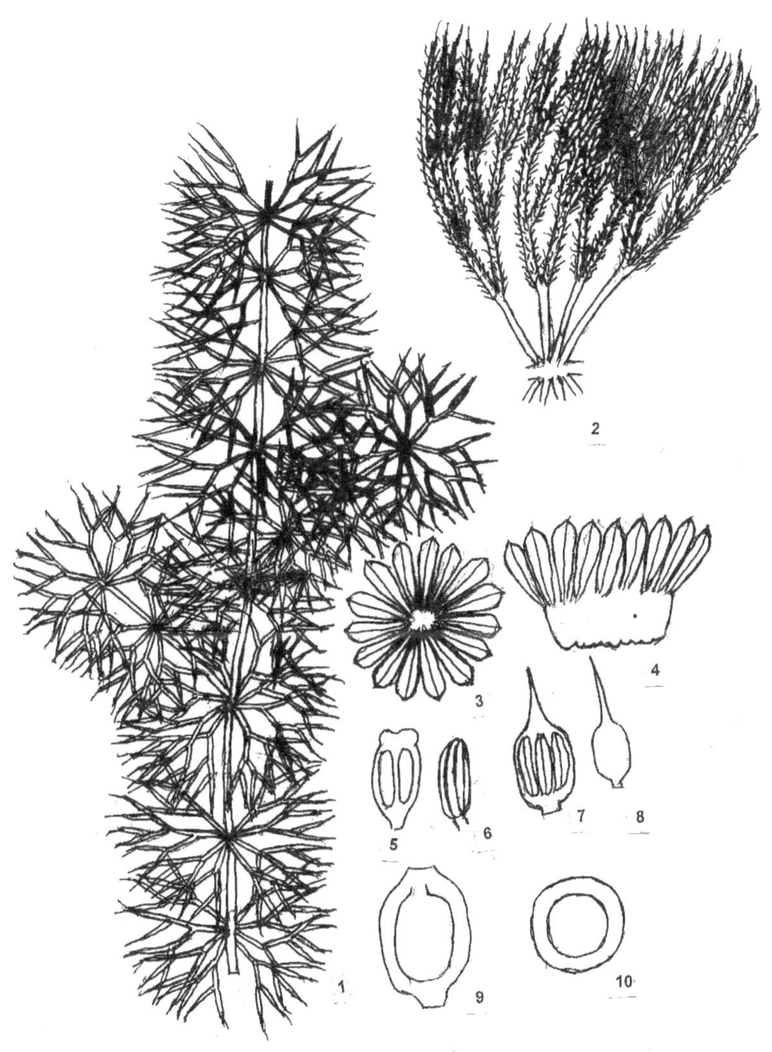

Plate 9   *Ceratophyllum demersum;* **Figure** 1 = A plant; 2 = Leaves; 3 and 4 = Perianth lobes; 5 to 8 = stamens and carpel 9 and 10 = L.S. and T.S. Ovary

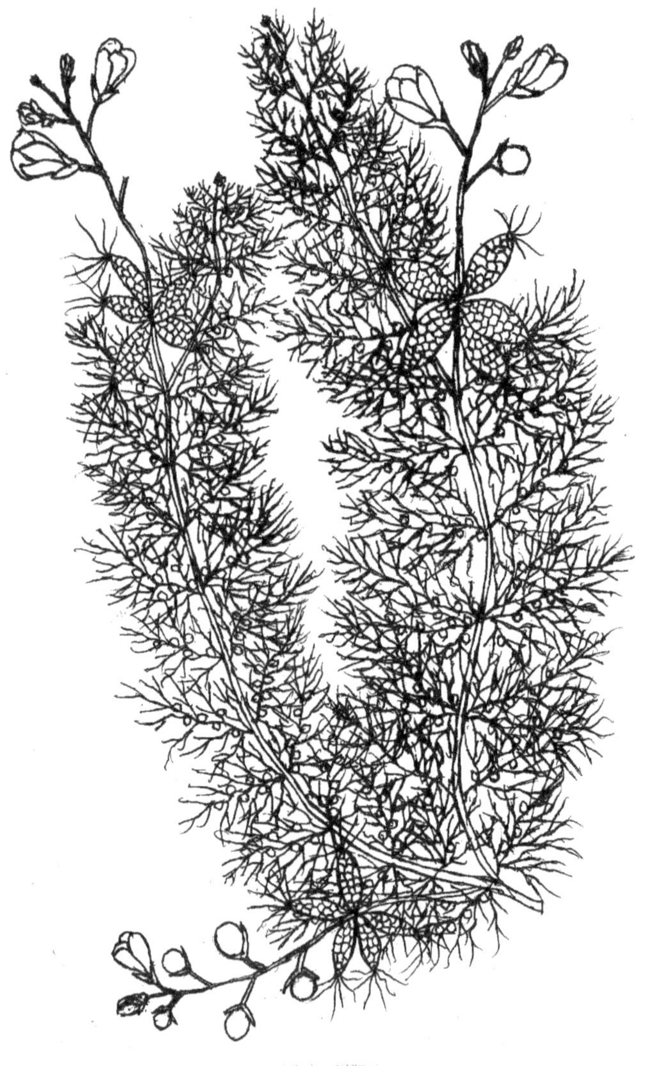

Plate 10 *Utricularia stellaris*

Plate 11   *Lymnophyton obtusifolium;* **Figure** 1 = A plant; 2 = Male flower; 3 = Female flower; 4 and 5 = Sepal and petal; 6 = Stamen; 7 = Carpel; 8 and 9 = L.S and T.S. Ovary.

Plate 12 *Monochoria vaginalis;* **Figure** 1 = A plant; 2 = Flower; 3 = Petals with stamens; 4 = Pistil; 5 = Stamens; 6 and 7 = L.S. and T.S. Ovary.

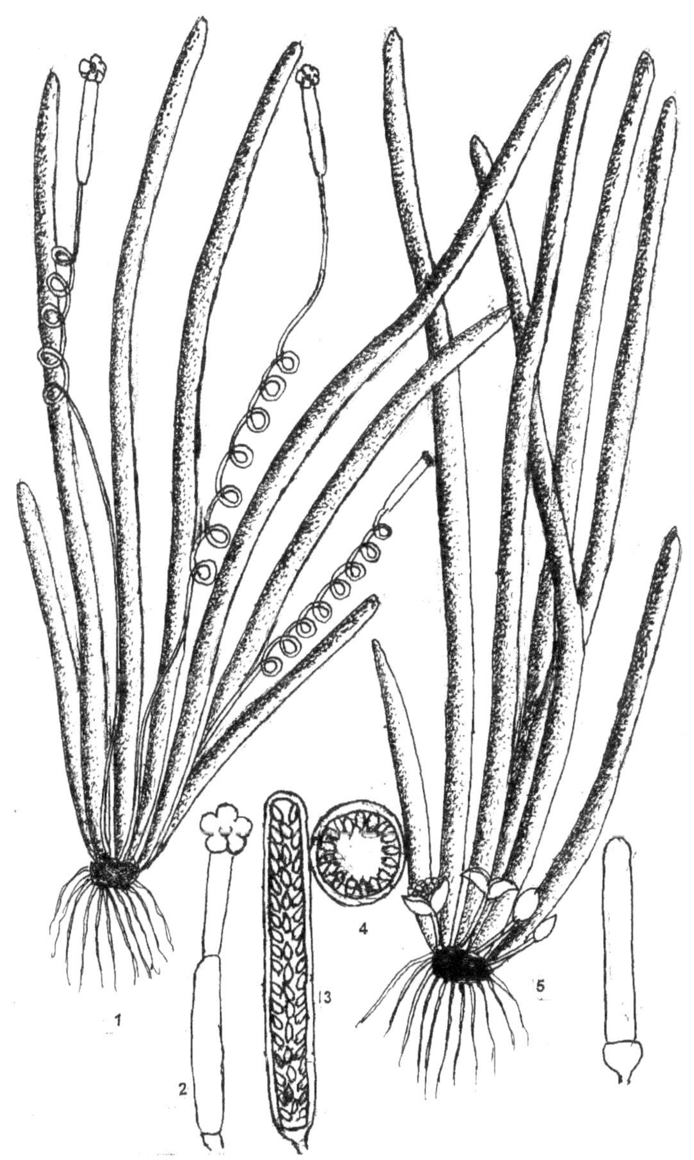

Plate 13 *Vallisneria spiralis;* **Figure** 1 = Female plant; 2 = Female flowers; 3 and 4 = L.S. and T.S. Ovary; 5 = Male plant.

Plate 14 *Blyxa octandra;* Figure 1 = A plant; 2 = Male flowers; 3 = Pistillode; 4 to 6 = Perianth lobes; 7 = Stamens and Pistillodes; 8 = Fruit of **B. chlinosperma**

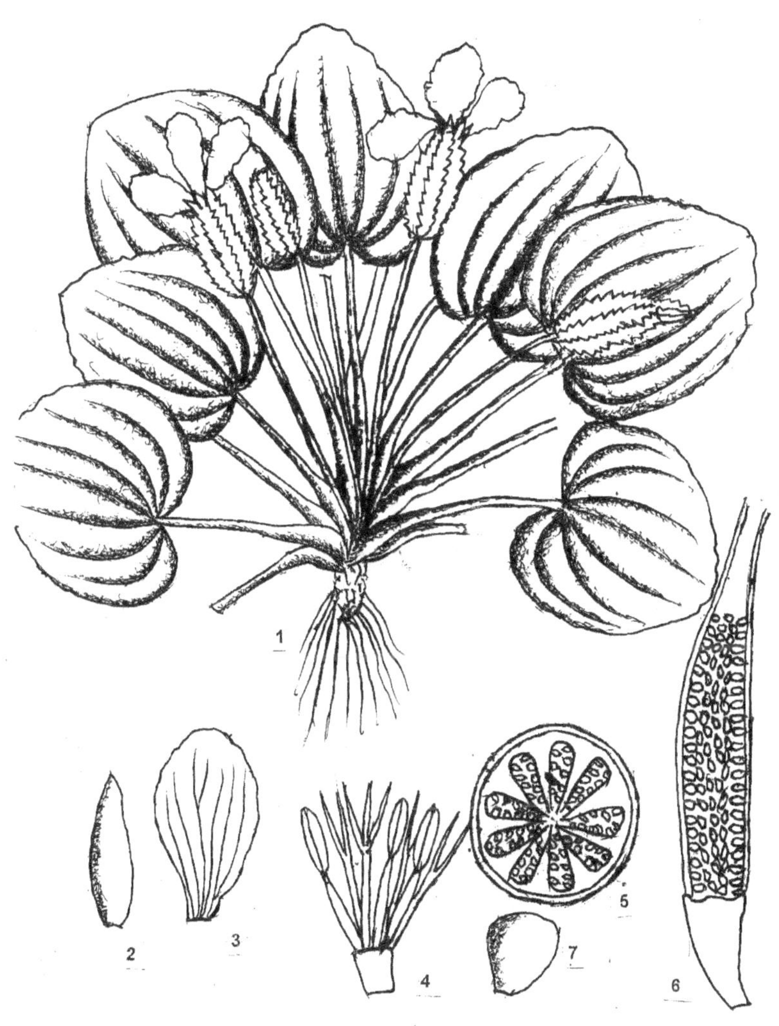

Plate 15 *Ottelia alismoides;* **Figure** 1 = A plant; 2 and 3 = perianth lobes; 4 = Stamens and Carpels; 5 and 6 = T.S. and L.S. Ovary; 7 = seed.

Plate 16   *Eichhornia crassipes;* **Figure** 1 = Plant; 2 = A flower, 3 and
4 = Stamens; 5 = carpel; 6 and 7 = L.S. and T.S. Ovary.

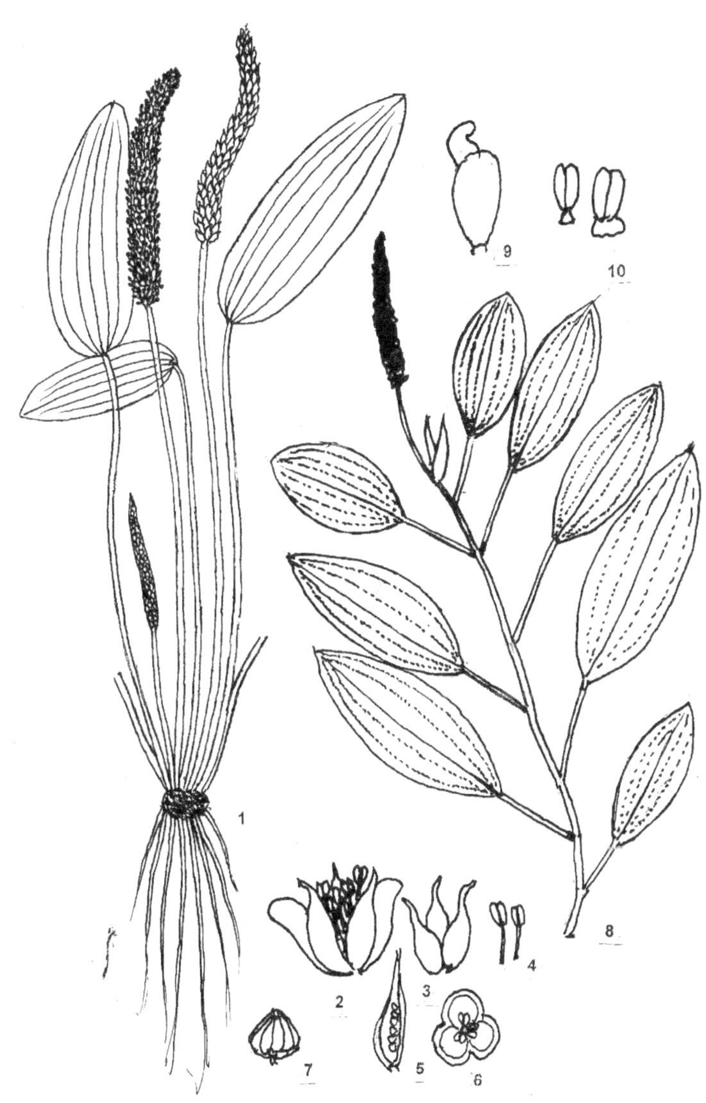

Plate 17   *Apanogeton natans;* **Figure** 1 = Plant; 2= Flower; 3 = Ovaries; 4 = Stamens; 5 and 6 = L.S. and T.S. Ovary; 7 = Fruit. **Figure** 8 to 10 = *Potamogeton nodosus;* **Figure** 8 = A plant; 9 = Pistil; 10 = Stamens.

2. HELOPHYTES

The plants of this group can live both inside water and on wet soil of the borders of water canals, ditches and small water reservoirs. These plants are comparable to animals which are amphibious, that they can live both inside water and on soil. Plants like *Typha* and *Pandanus* are always present either inside water of 1 or 2 feet depth or outside the water canals on the wet borders. But, these plants cannot grow in pure dry soil. The author likes to treat these plants under helophytes of Aquatic Angiosperms.

FAMILY 1: BALSAMINACEAE

There are 2 genera under this family. *Impatiens* is a large genus having more than 80 species in South India. The other genus is *Hydrocera* having a species *H. triflora* W&A. in Tamilnadu. The author has collected this species some 20 years back in the peripheral area of a water ditch in Poondiankuppam village of Cuddalore District. The basal stem is semiecret and roots are produced at the basal 4 to 5 nodes. The fruit is drupe and falls down at maturity.

FAMILY 2: FABACEAE (PAPILIONAECEAE)

Aeschenomene aspera L. and *A. indica*. L are the two plants of this family found on the borders of tanks and lakes. The stem of the latter species is used to prepare coloured garlands to cattle during pongal festival. The former species is floating on the water with 1 to 1½ feet depth. When the summer season starts up, these plants can live in wet soil for several days. If the soil gets dried up, these plants will perish with flowers and fruits.

FAMILY 3: ONAGRACEAE

In marshes and small ditches *Ludwigia adscendens* **(Plate - 3)** L. H. Hara (*Jussieaua repens.*, L) is present during rainy season on the borders of ditches and the branches are floating on the surface of water with the help of small air bladders present in the axils of stem. The other species of this family is also helophytic. When the soil gets dried up, these plants cannot live in that place.

FAMILY 4: BUDDLEJACEAE

Buddleja asiatica Lour. is a helophyte, 1½ feet high with weak stem, more branched, present in marshes and wet soil with little water in water canals during rainy season. The author has noted this species from Sethiathope to Bhuvanagiri in a water canal by the side of bus route to Chidambaram. This is the only member of this family in the plains of Tamil nadu.

FAMILY 5: APIACEAE (UMBELLIFERALE)

Centella asiatica L., **(Plate - 5)** is a small spreading herb on the wet soil of ditches and water canals. The leaves are medicinally important. Now a days, it is fast disappearing from the earth due to human disturbances and unfavourable climatic conditions.

FAMILY 6: GENTIANACEAE

Enicostemma littorale (Willd.) L.Verd., *Exacum pedunculatum* L. and *Canscora diffusa* Linn. are the water loving plants of this family. They are present on the borders of paddy fields when there is enough water during the rainy seasons. These plants cannot live in dry soil.

FAMILY 7: CONVOLVULACEAE

Ipomoea carnea Linn. is a helophyte, 4 to 5 feet high, freely branched with pink or purple flowers, present on the borders of water canals, ditches and lakes. The leaves are used to make garlands and the flowers are showy.

Ipomea sepiaria J. Koeniq ex. Roxb. is another plant found on the borders of water canals and lakes. But the main stem is running on water inside, 4 to 5 meters length and making a complete covering. The leaves are green, found to be edible and have some medicinal value. The flowers are large, pink coloured and showy.

FAMILY 8: ACANTHACEAE

Hygrophila balsamica (Lf) Ref **(Plate - 10)** (*Cardanthera verticillata*) and *H. spinosa* L. (*Asteracantha lonifolia* (L.) Nees.) are the two more commonly occurring water loving plants during the rainy seasons. They are present in wet and marshy places with thin film of water. During the onset of summer, they disappear.

FAMILY 9: SCROPHULARIACEAE

Angelonia biflora (*Angelonia grandiflora* Benth) **(Plate - 9)** is a beautiful plant present on the borders of ditches and lakes. They form a compact colony of 20 to 40 plants in a particular place. Flowers are violet, large and showy.

Lymnophila heterophylla Merr **(Plate - 9)** is another wild plant of this family always present in the water ditches, paddy fields and shallow water waste lands. The submerged leaves are dissected and hairy but the leaves above the water level are entire.

The other helophytic species are:

1)   *Ammannia baccifera – Lythraceae*

2)   *A. octandra – Lythraceae*

These two species are Lythraceae members present in wet paddy fields with thin film of water. The other Scrophulariaceae members are:

3)   *Stemodia viscosa*

4)   *Sopubia trifida*

5)   *Scoparia dulcis*

6)   *Microcarpaea muscosa*, R.Br.

7)   *Micrargeria wightii*. Benth.

8)   *Lindernia tenuifolia* (Colsm) Alston

9)   *L. crustacea* (L) F.Muell (*Vandelia crustacea* (L) Benth

10) *L. hyssopioides* (L) Axines

11) *L. oppositifolia* (Retz) Mukerjee.

12) *L. ciliata* (Colsm.)Pennell.

13) *L. anagallis (Burm.f.)* Pennell.

14) *Dopatrium lobelioides* Benth.

15) *D. nudicanule* Buch – Ham

16) *Bacopa monnieri* (L) Westtst. (*Moniera cuneifolia*)
     (Plate - 9)

17) *Lymnophila chinensis* (Osbeck) Merr. (*L. hirsuta* Benth)
     (Plate - 9).

18) *L. indica* (L) Druce

19) *L. polystachya* Benth

20) *L. parviflora* (Roxb) Haines

21) *Aneilima esculentum* Wall

This last species is a Commelinaceae member present in paddy fields. The species of *Lymnophila, Dopatrium* and *Lindernia* require water stagnant clay soil or at least thin film of water on loose soil for their living. They produce roots at the basal 3 to 4 nodes of main stem all around and these roots reach the loose soil and penetrate to absorb water and nutrients. These plants are weak or fleshy stemmed, semierect small herbs or almost spreading on the soil so that the roots at the basal nodes may get easy attachment on the soil. They have minute or small leaves and produce a large number of small or minute fruits. Within the rainy season, they complete their life cycle. They will be present on the borders of paddy fields and after the harvest of paddy, they will perish. In the next rainy season, they start growing in the same places and this is a continuous process.

The use of most of these wild but beautiful plants is not completely known. Each plant should have appeared in this earth with a purpose but our knowledge is insufficient to understand their purpose of creation and living in this earth. Most of these plants belong to the family Scrophulariaceae and Gentianaceae. Another helophytic family is Ranunculaceae but it is a family of hill station plants (living at 5000 to 8500 feet altitudes of Ooty, Kodaikanal and Valparai). All these 3 families are considered as more important families of flowering plants with large number of ornamental plants. Even the wild plants are more beautiful in these families.

There are several plants intermediate between Hydrophytes and Helophytes on one hand and between Helophytes and Terrestrial plants on the other.

Cleome chelidonii of Capparidaceae, starts its life first as a helophyte but finishes its life as a terrestrial plant. The other examples are *Commelina bengalensis* Linn. and *C. nudiflora* Linn. There are several members of Cyperaceae and Graminaceae in the plain areas following this transitional life. But they are considered now as terrestrial plants. *Aneilima esculentum* Wall is a helophyte of Commelinaeceae living along with paddy in the plains of Tamilnadu.

FAMILY 10: HYDROPHYLLACEAE

Hydrolea zeylanica (L.) **(Plate - 7)** Vahl. is a marsh living plant. The stem is repeatedly branched and prostrate on the wet soil making a thick green car pet. Over it, there are a large number of blue flowers. It is beautiful even though it is wild in Tamil Nadu. In dry soil we cannot grow them, even though sufficient water is supplied to them.

FAMILY 11: ARACEAE

Colocasia antiquorum Schott; among a few varieties, there is a wild variety of this species present on the borders of water canals, ditches and small lakes. These plants make distinct colonies.

FAMILY 12: AMARANTHACEAE

Alternanthera sessilis (L.) R.Br. Ex. Dc (*A. triandra* Linn.). **(Plate - 12)**. It is growing under thin film of water on the borders of water canals. They require pure water. Sometimes, in wet soil, they make dense colonies. The leaves are cooked and eaten by village people and it is one of the more important medicinal plants to cure eye defects. It is called in Tamil "Ponnankanni".

FAMILY 13: POLYGONACEAE

Polygonum glabrum Willd **(Plate - 14)** and *Persicaria barbata* (L.) H. Hars **(Plate - 15)** (*Polygonum barbatum* Linn.) are the two plants of this family which always grow by the side of water resources. They are not found in the dry soil. Both these species make dense colonies of 3 to 4 feet in height. The flowers in terminal spikes in *Polygonum glabrum* are pinkish-red and very beautiful.

FAMILY 14: AMARYLLIDACEAE

The wild species of *Crinum* namely *C. defixum* **(Plate - 18)** Ker. and *C.latifolium Linn* are growing on the borders of water canals and ditches. The globular bulbs of these species are buried under the soil and the leaves and cluster of white flowers in long pedicelled inflorescences are present above the soil. They are not available during summer or in dry cultivated soil. They are also medicinally important.

FAMILY 15: TYPHACEAE

Typha angustata Bory and Chaub. **(Plate - 21)** is a wild species in Tamil Nadu. It is always present in colonies on the borders of water canals or inside water up to a depth of 2 to 3 feet during the rainy seasons. Plants are 5 to 6 feet length with narrow thin and long leaves. The leaves are cut and spread on the ground on the way to marriage hall during marriage functions. The dried leaves are used to prepare mats and other household things. The pearl millet is resembling those plants, so it is named as "*Pennisetum typhoides*". They can live in wet soil for many days.

FAMILY 16: PANDANACEAE

Pandanus odoratissimus L.f. **(Plate - 20)** is a wild species in Tamilnadu. Some 60 years back when the author was studying in high school, there were *Pandanus* thickets covering 10 to 20 acres land, on the borders of a large lake on the eastern side of his village, Ko-Athanur, of Virudhachalam Taluk as a small forest. On the southern sides of the village also there were small group of plants. From 1960 onwards these plants started disappearing and now, there is not a single plant in his village. Due to reduced rain fall and human disturbances, these plants gradually disappeared. These plants are useful in multi various ways to human beings and the white large flower spikes are highly scented and more beautiful. Now a days, these plants are fast disappearing and we have to take suitable conservation methods not only to save the remaining plants but also to establish them in more numbers.

FAMILY 17: CYPERACEAE (PLATES – 21 TO 31)

Some of the species of *Cyperus* are found on the borders of water canals and wet rice fields during rainy season. On the starting of summer, these plants disappear. In the dry soil, these plants will not live. Important helophytic species of this family in Tamil Nadu plains are *Scirpus squarrosus* L., *Pseudomariscus cyperoides* (Rottb.) *Rauschert; Cyperus difformis. L., C. castaneus. Willd, C. corymbosus Rottb., Eleocharis dulcis (Burm.f). Henschel, E.spiralis (Rottb.) Roemer and schultes; Schoenoplectus senegalensis, (Hochst. ex. Steud.) Palla; S.spiralis (Rottb.)* Roemer and Schultes; *S. juncoides* (Roxb) Palla; *S.lateriflorus* (J. F. Gmelin) Lye; *S.littoralis* (Schrader) Palla; *S. articulatus* (L.) Palla and *S.mucronatus* (L) Palla.

The other helophytic members of Cyperaceae in the plains of Tamil Nadu are:

1) *Cyperus rotundus* Linn. (Plate)

2) *Cyperus haspen* Linn. (Plate)

3) *Cyperus laevigatus* L. (*Juncelus laevigatus* (L)

4) *Cyperus compresses* Linn,

5) *Cyperus iria* L.

6) *Cyperus procerus* Rottb.

7) *Cyperus articulates* Linn

8) *Cyperus platistylis* R.Br.

9) *Cyperus tenuispica* Steud

10) *Cyperus castaneus* wild

11) *Cyperus pangori* Rottb

12) *Cyperus corymbosus* Rottb.

13) *Cyperus exaltatus* Retz

14) *Cyperus triceps* Endl. (*Kyllinga triceps* Rottb.) (Plate)

15) *Eleocharis spiralis* (Rottb) Roemer and Schultes

16) *Eleocharis dulcis* (Burm.f) Henschel

17) *Eleocharis congesta*

18) *Eleocharis atropurpureus* (Retz.) C., Presl

19) *Eleocharis acutangula* (Roxb) Schultes. (*E.fistulosa* Schultes)

20) *Eleocharis geniculata* (L)

21) *Eleocharis retroflexa* (Poiret)

22) *Eleocharis plantaginea* R.Br.

23) *Eleocharis capitata* R.Br.

24) *Eleocharis chaetaria* Roemer & Schultes

25) *Eleocharis tetraquetra* Nees

26) *Fimbristylis bisumbellata* Bub

27) *Bulbeostylis barbata*

28) *Pseudomariscus cyperoides* Rauschert. (*Courtoisia cyperoides*, Roxb.)

29) *Pycreus pumilus*

30) *Schoenoplectus lateriflorus* (Plate)

31) *Schoenoplectus articulates* Linn (Plate)

32) *Schoenoplectus mucronatus*

33) *Schoenopleclus senegalensis* Fischer (Plate)

34) *Schoenoplectus supinus* Linn **(Plate)**.

35) *Scirpus grossus* Linn.

It is clear that most of the species of *Cyperus*, *Eleocharis* and *Schoenoplectus* of Cyperaceae family in Tamil Nadu plains are living in marshy or foggy habitats or in rice fields and stagnant water or flowing regions during the rainy seasons. These plants are not found in pure terrestrial habitats or dry lands of Tamil Nadu. On the onset of summer they will be found for a few days in wet soil and then perish.

On the other hand there are some Cyperaceae members which can live in dry soil throughout the life with available rain water or intermittent irrigations among the cultivated crops.

But it is difficult sometimes to separate a helophyte from terrestrial plants, because of overlapping characters present in some of the Cyperaceae members. Therefore, it is a trial and error to solve the problems of this categorization.

There is another problem incoming to the ecological status of paddy. Now-a-days, along with higher yielding and better quality crops, disease resistant and drought tolerant varieties of paddy have been introduced continuously. Some of the non-irrigated varieties, that is, monsoon varieties are available now in paddy. At the same time there is continuous supply of water from the seedling stage upto harvest level in most of the varieties of paddy. Therefore paddy can live in water as well as in wet soil. But it cannot live in dry soil. Therefore, the author is inclined to keep it as a helophyte instead of hydrophyte or terrestrial plant.

FAMILY 18: POACEAE (GRAMINEAE) (PLATES 32 AND 33)

Some of the species are growing inside the thin film of water or on the borders of water canals and small streams like *Saccharum spontaneum* Linn. Plants like *Leersia hexandra* Sw. and *Hygrorhiza aristata* Nees, *Oryza meyeriana* Brill., *O. coarctata* Roxb., *Hymenachne pseudointerrupta* C. Muell, are helophytes in the plains of Tamil Nadu. According to Gamble (1957), *Leersia hexandra* is living from mean sea level to 7000 feet elevations of hill stations. *Leersia* and *Ophiorhiza* are more related to paddy and the fruit grains of these species are more resembling to those of *Oryza sativa*. Therefore, the species of *Oryza*, *Leersia* and *Ophiorhiza* may be considered as helophytes.

Oryza glabrescens is a wild paddy in Tamil nadu. The author has seen it some 10 years back on the border of a small ditch among the paddy fields near Khan saheeb water canal, Chidambaram. It is on the northern side of Chidambaam near Manalur. It is a colony of 10 to 30 plants as a clump, semierect and the panicle has black fruits with long awns. As soon as they mature they fall down, mostly inside water. The fruits are as large as the cultivated paddy fruits, particularly "ponmani" variety.

When the author travelled to north India by trains he would see another wild paddy *Oryza meyeriana* in small ditches with stagnant water of 1 to 2 feet high by the sides of railway lines between Ponneri to Guduvanchery, north to Madras on the way to Andhrapradesh. The panicles are longer and the fruits red coloured and the fruits are as large as those of "Vellai Ponni" variety of cultivated paddy.

Another wild paddy, *Oryza coarctata,* a mangrove associate, is rarely present in the mangrove forests of Kille and Pichavaram. The author has seen it some 20 years back on the borders of back water canals near the sea shore of Bay of Bengal at Kille, Chidambaram. The diagram of this plant has been provided in Part I "Mangrove Flora" of the "Flowering plants of Tamil Nadu", already published by the author.

Leersia hexandra has the capacity to live inside water, 1 to 2 feet depth as well as in wet soil for many days. The height of the plants depends upon the depth of water in a particular place. The plants present in wet soil are dwarf, bushy and dark green and produce large number of inflorescences, when compared to the plants present inside water.

Hygrorhiza aristata is very rare in Tamil Nadu and it has adaptive mechanisms to float on the surface of water upto a few feet length.

The other water living Gramineae members are:

1) *Imperata cylindrica Beauv.* (Tharpai pullu)

2) *Saccharum spontaneum* Linn. (Nanal)

3) *Rottboellia exaltata* Linn.

4) *Eriochloa procera* C.E. Hubbard.

5) *Paspalidium punctatum* A Camus

6) *P. geminatum* Stapf

7) *Echinochloa crus-galli* Beauv.

8) *E. stagnina* Beauv.

9) *Pseudoraphis aspera* Pilger.

10) *Isachne dispar* Trin (Nellu Millatthi)

11) *Arundinella lawsonii* Hook f. and

12) *Arundo donax* Linn.

Fischer and Gamble (1957) have enumerated 387 species including some varieties under 132 genera of this grass family. There are a large number of hill station plants at higher attitudes in neighbouring states of India, in mangrove vegetations and in the hot and drier areas of Tamil nadu. Only 16 species are helophytes living in and near water resources. Therefore, grasses are mostly terrestrial plants. On the other hand, Cyperaceae members are mostly helophytes.

In the grass family, there are a large number of cultivated plants. But in Cyperaceae only a few species are cultivated for multivarious purposes, and not as food grains.

There are 20 genera of Cyperaceae having 170 species and a few varieties. Therefore this family along with the grasses represent the larger group of flowering plants.

Eriocaulaceae members are related to Cyperaceae members but very simple in appearance. They are mostly cool loving plants. Of the 27 species enumerated by Fischer and Gamble (1957), most of them are present in Karnataka and at higher altitudes of hill stations of Western Ghats. Only a few species are present in the plains of Tamil Nadu but they are not considered as helophytes.

Pentapetes phoenicea **(Plate-1)**, *Aeschynomene indica*, *A. aspera*, some convolvulaceae, Gentianaceae, Eacphorliaceae, *Hydrocera triflora* and Araceae are also members of Helophytes **(Plates 10, 11, 12 and 13).**

EXPLANATIONS OF PLATES AND FIGURES

HELOPHYTES

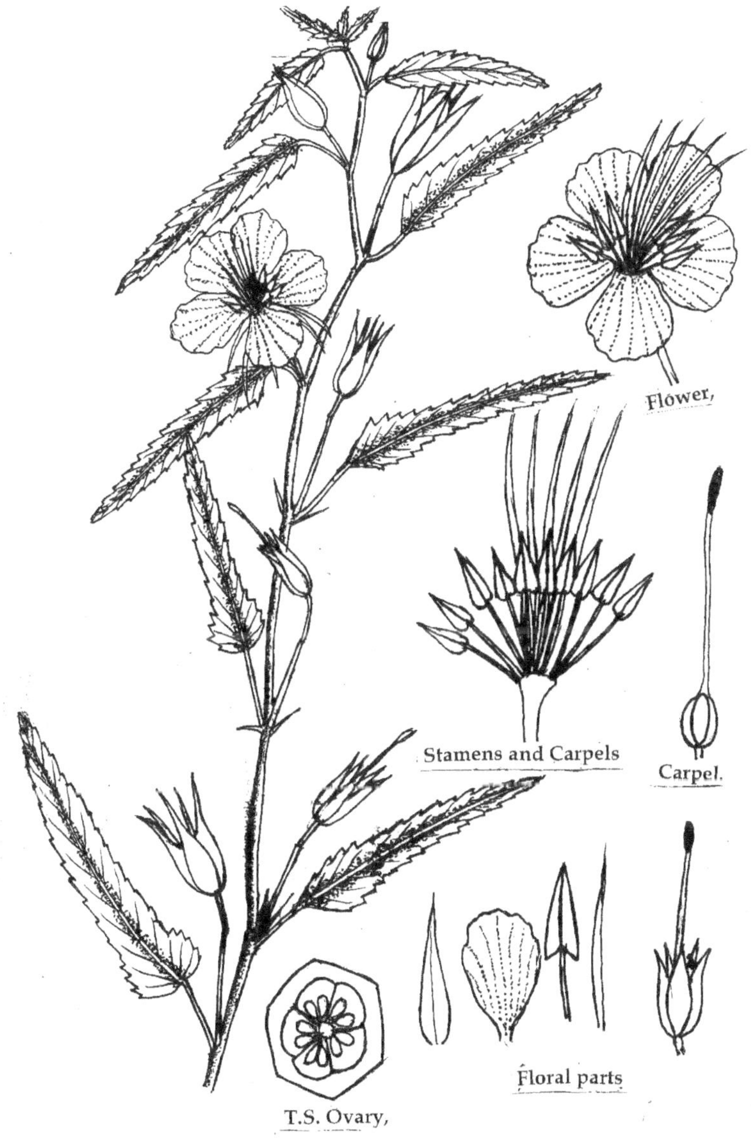

Plate 1 *Pentapetes phoenicea*

Plate 2 *Ludwigia suffruiticosa;* **Figure** 1 = A branch, 2 = A flower; 3 = L.S. Flower; 4 = Fruit; 5 to 8 = Floral parts; 9 = T.S. Ovary

Plate 3   **Figure** 1 to 6 = ***Ludwigia perennis;*** **Figure** 1 = A plant; 2= flower; 3 = Stamens; 4 = Carpel; 5 and 6 = L.S and T.S. Ovary. **Figure:** 7 to 12 = ***Ludwigia adscendens;*** **Figure:** 7 = A twig; 8 = Flower; 9 = Stamens; 10 = Carpel; 11 and 12 = L.S. and T.S. Ovary.

Plate 4 **Figure** 1 to 7 = ***Waltheria indica* var. *kapperensis;* Figure** 1 = A plant; 2 = Flower; 3 = Sepals; 4 = Petal; 5 = Carpel; 6 = Stamen; 7 = T.S. Ovary. **Figure** 8 to 13 = ***Melochia corchorifolia;* Figure** 8 = A plant; 9 = Flower; 10 = Sepals; 11 = Petal; 12 = Carpel; 13 = T.S.Ovary

Plate 5   *Centella asiatica*; **Figure** 1 = Plant; 2 = Spathe; 3 = Flower, 4 = Fruits; 5 = Petal; 6 = sepal, 7 = stamens; 8 and 9 = L.S. and T.S. Ovary; 10 = Dehisced fruit.

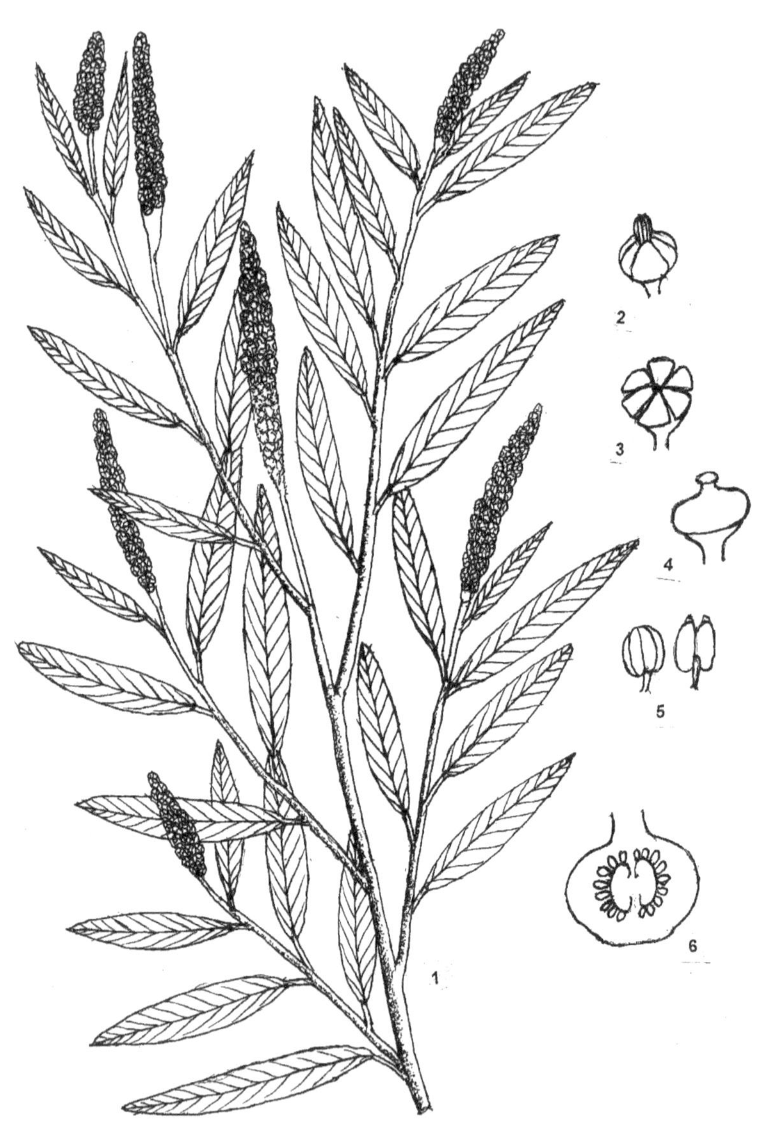

Plate 6   *Sphenoclea zeylanica;* **Figure** 1 = A plant; 2 = A flower; 3 = Fruit; 4 = Ovary; 5 = Stamens; 6 = L.S.Ovary.

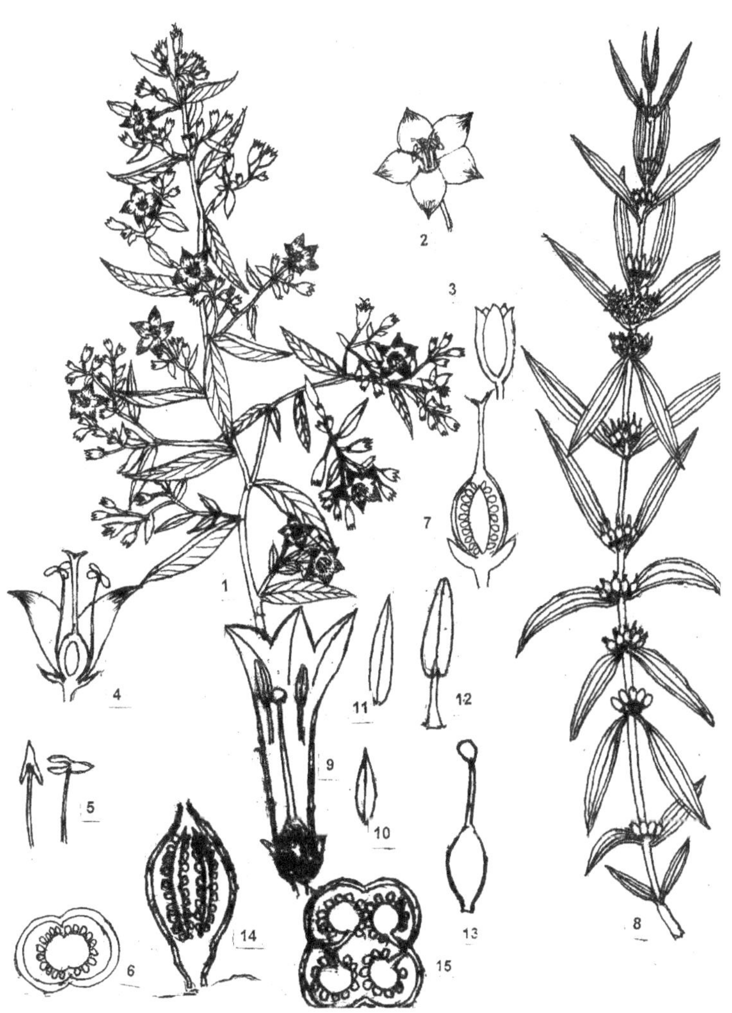

Plate 7 **Figure** 1 to 7 = **Hydrolea zeylanica; Figure** 1 = A twig; 2 = A flower; 3 = A fruit; 4 = M.L.S. Flower; 5 = Stamens; 6 and 7 = T.S. and L.S. Ovary. **Figure** 8 to 15 = ***Enicostemma littorale; Figure*** 8 = A plant; 9 = M.L.S. Flower; 10=Sepal; 11=petal; 12=stamens; 13=carpel; 14 and 15 = L.S,. and T.S.Ovary.

Plate 8 *Barringtonia acutangula;* Figure 1 = A branch; 2=Flower; 3 to 5 = Floral parts; 6=Fruit; 7 and 8 = T.S. and L.S. Ovary.

Plate 9   **Figures 1 to 3.** *Becopa moneirii;* **Figure** 1 = plant; 2 = Flower; 3 = T.S. of flower; **Figure 4 to 7** = *Angelonia biflora;* **Figure** 4 = A twig; 5 = Flower; 6 = M.L.S. Flower; 7 = Stamens; **Figure** 8 to 10 = *Lymnophila heterophylla;* Figure 8 = A plant; 9=A flower; 10 = L.S. and T.S. Ovary

Plate 10   **Figure** 1 to 5 = *Hygrophila balsamica;* **Figure** 1 = A plant; 2 = A flower; 3 = Stamens; 4 and 5 = L.S. and T.S. Ovary. **Figure** 6 to 9 = *Hygrophila auriculata,* **Figure** 6 = A twig; 7 = Flowers; 8 = carpel; 9 = stamens.

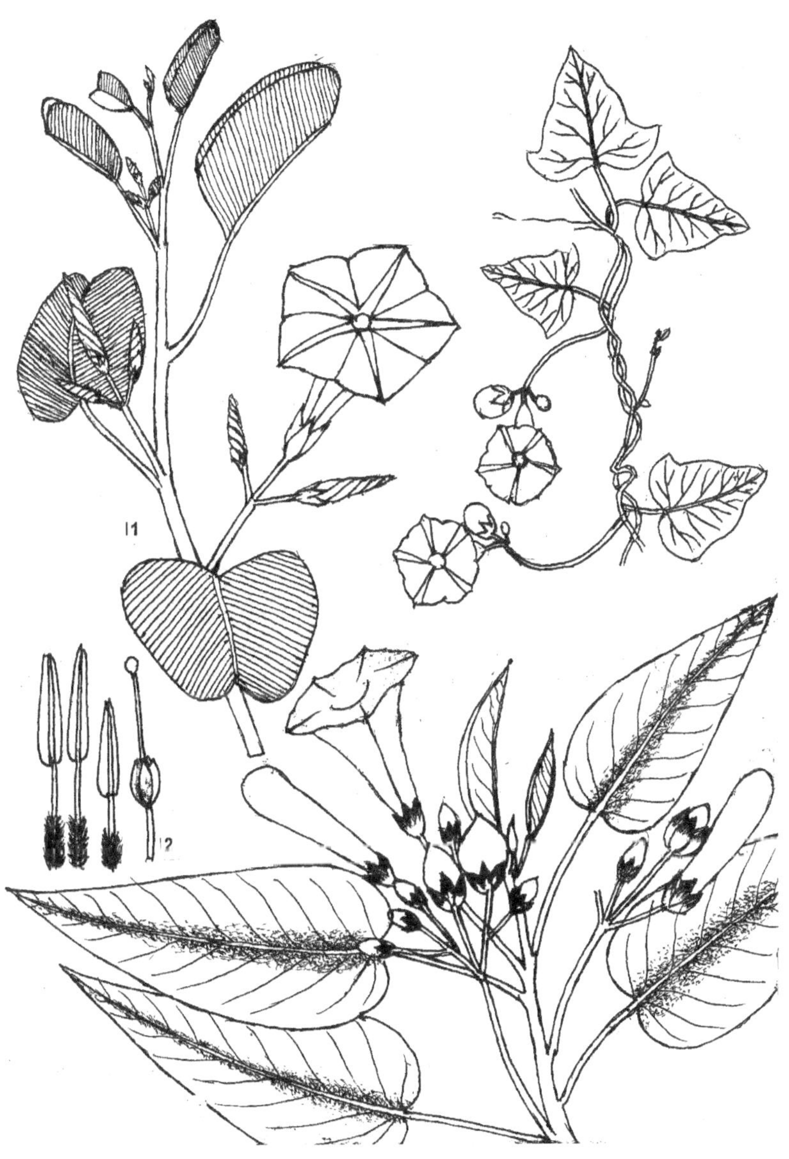

Plate 11 **Figure** 1 & 2 = *Ipomea biloba;* **Figure** 1 = A twig; 2 = Stamens and Carpel; **Figure** 3 = *Ipomea sepiaria;* **Figure** 4 = *Ipomea carnea*

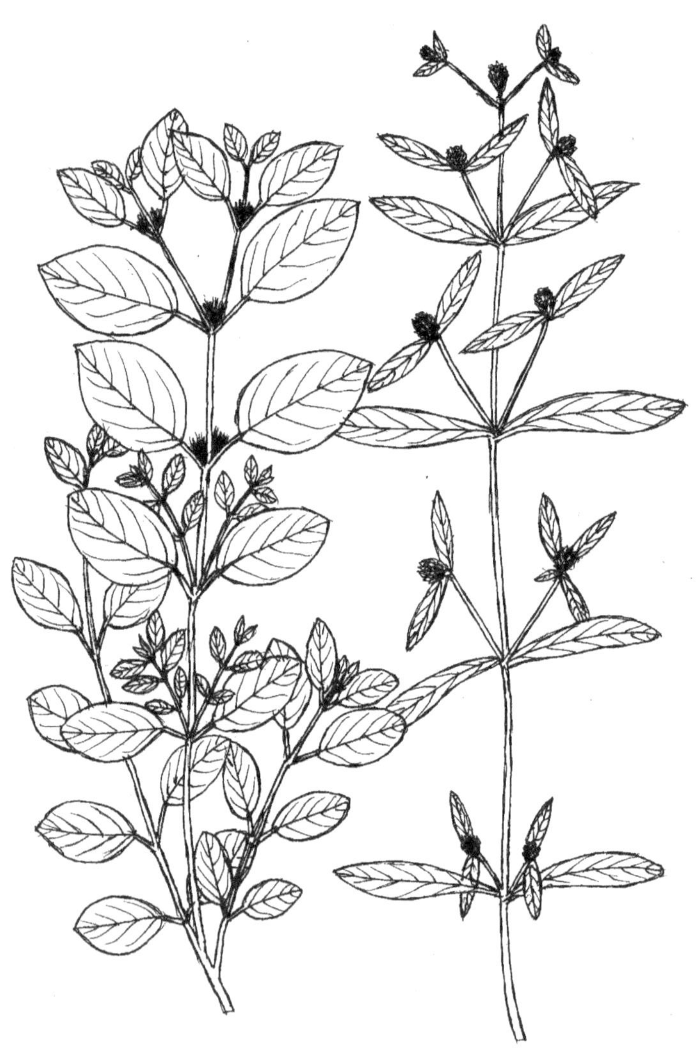

Plate 12 Figure 1 = *Psilotrichum elliotii;* **Figure 2** = *Alternanthera sessilis*

Plate 13 **Figure 1 to 7 = *Agynela bacciforme;*** 1 = A twig; 2 and 3 = Male flowers; 4 and 5 = Female flowers; 6 = T.S. Ovary; 7 = Fruit. **Figure** 8 to 14 = ***Pouzolzia auriculata;* Figure** 8 = A twig; 9 = Male flower; 10 = Female flower; 11 = Stamens 12 and 13 = L.S. and T.S. Ovary; 14 = A fruit.

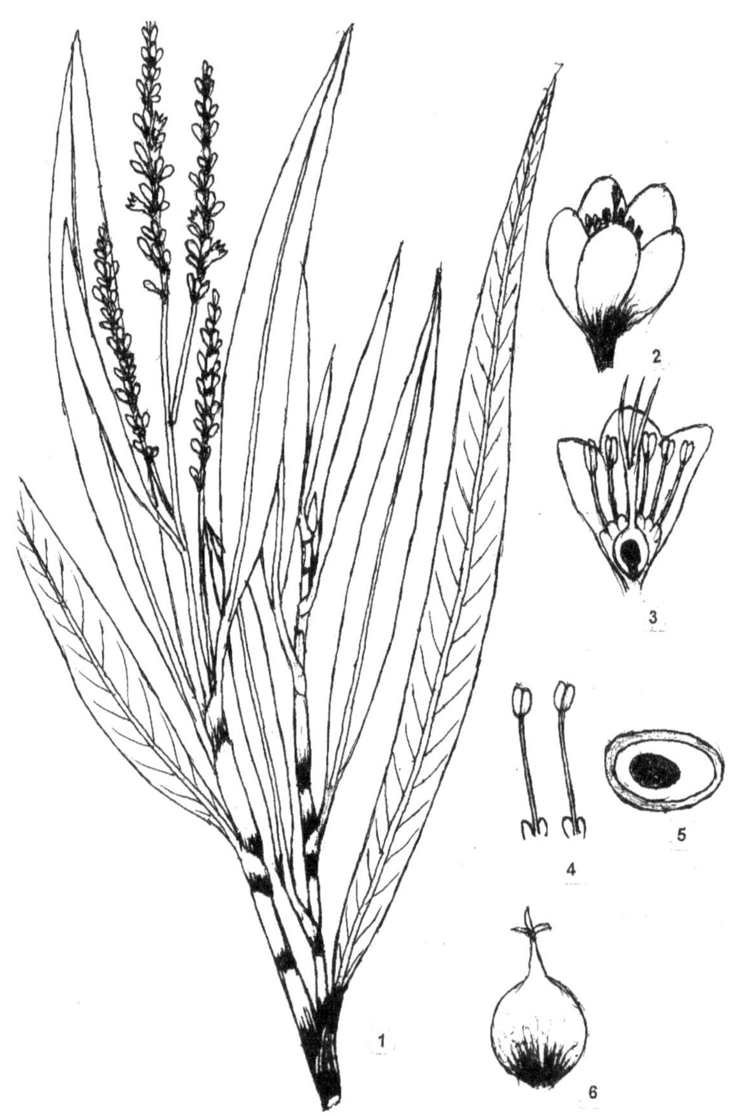

Plate 14 *Polygonum glabrum;* **Figure** 1 = A branch; 2 = A flower; 3 = M.L.S. Flower; 4 = Stamens; 5 = T.S. Ovary; 6 = Ovary.

Plate 15 *Persicaria barbata;* **Figure** 1 = A branch; 2 and 3 = Flowers; 4 = Stem.

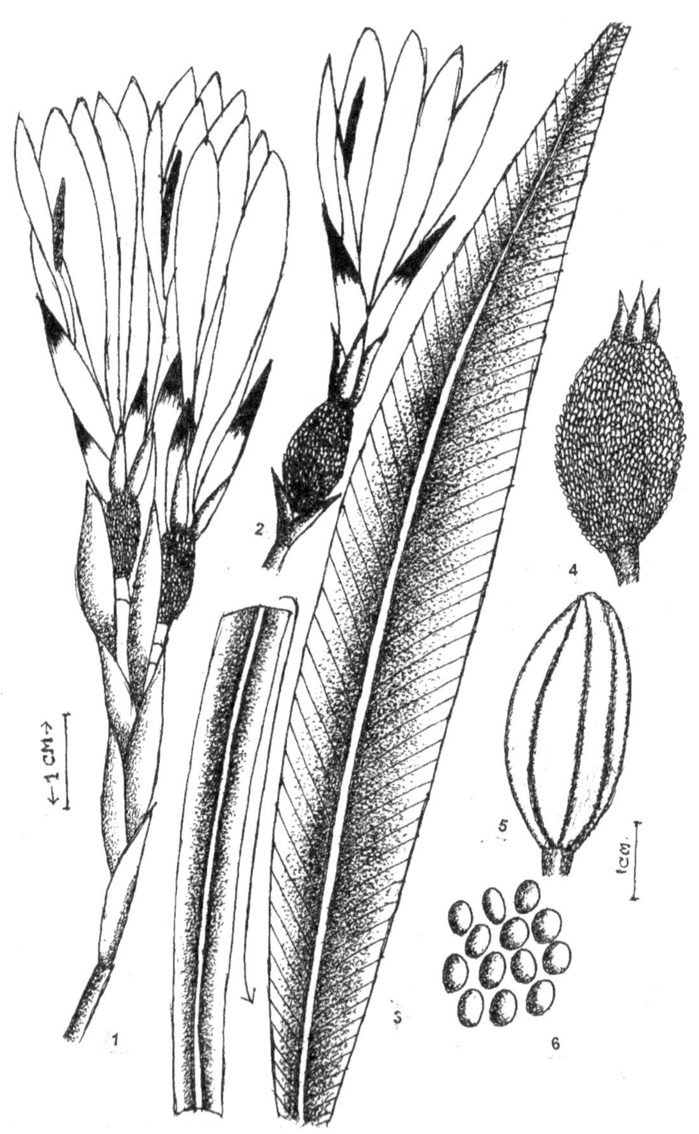

Plate 16 *Canna grandiflora* ; **Figure** 1 = Flower twig; 2 = Flower; 3 = A leaf; 4 and 5 = Young and Old fruits; 6 = seeds.

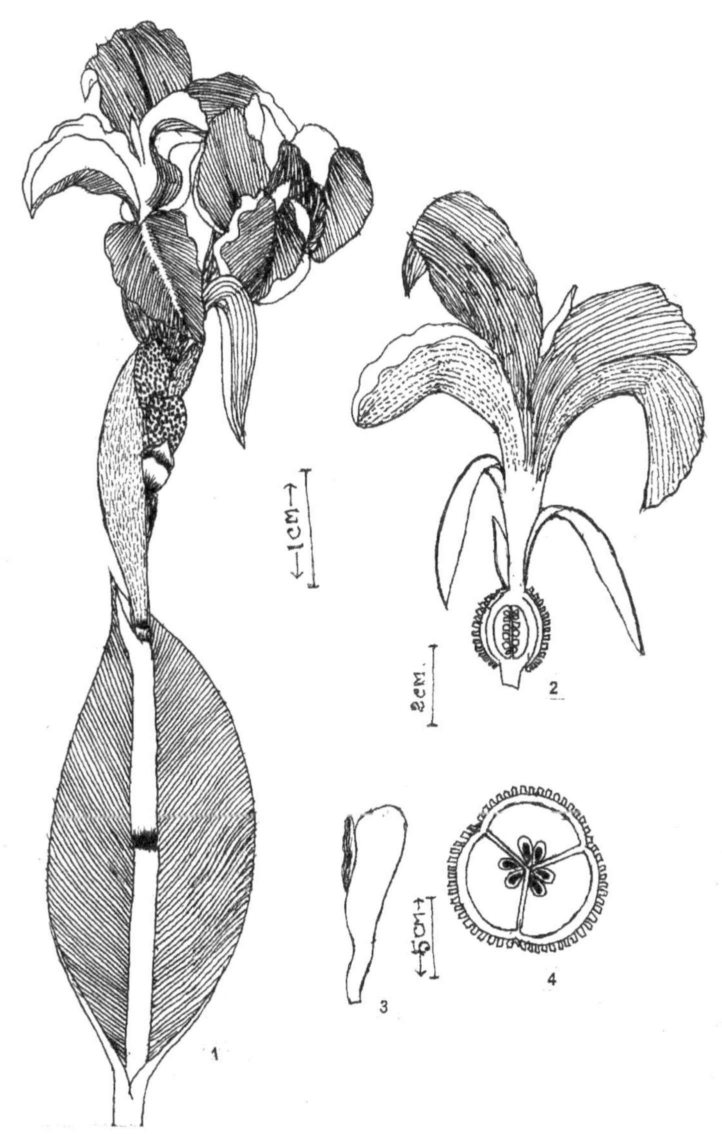

Plate 17 *Canna generalis*; **Figure** 1 = Twig; 2 = M.L.S. Flower; 3 = Stamen; 4 = T.S. Ovary

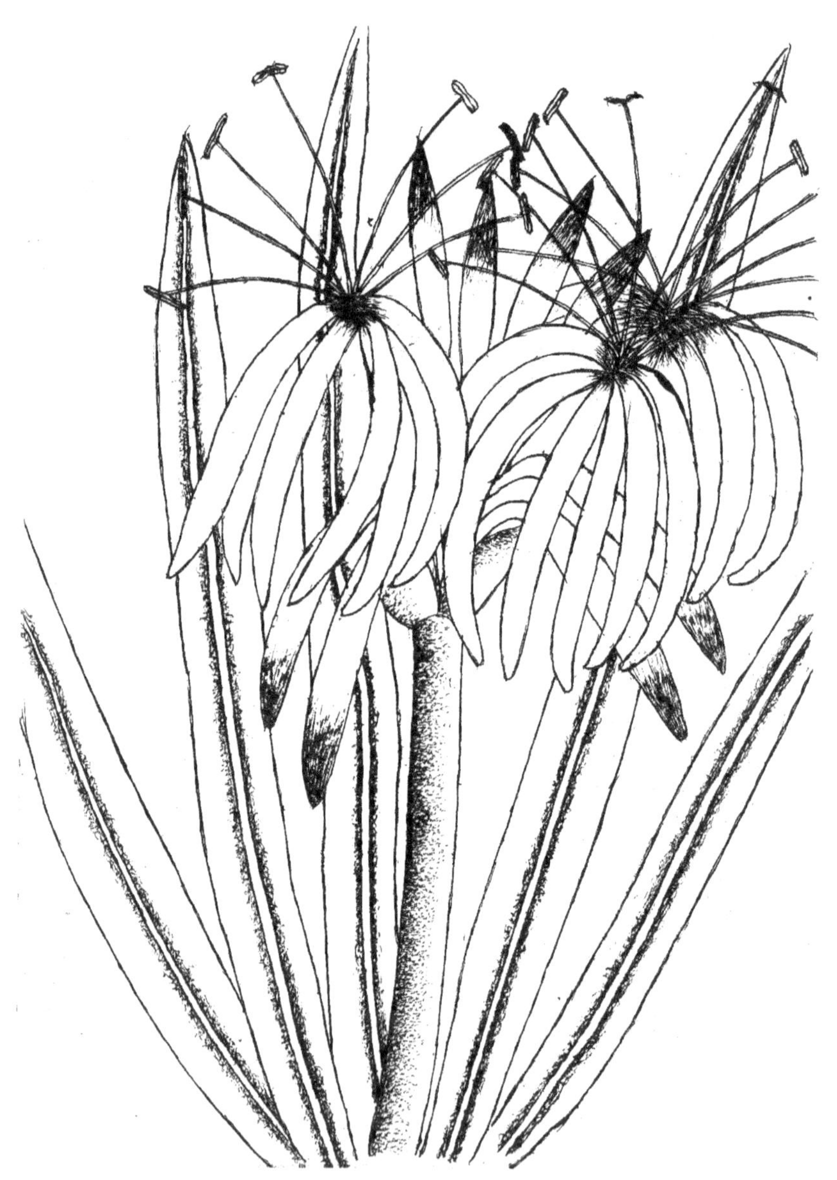

Plate 18   *Crinum defixum*

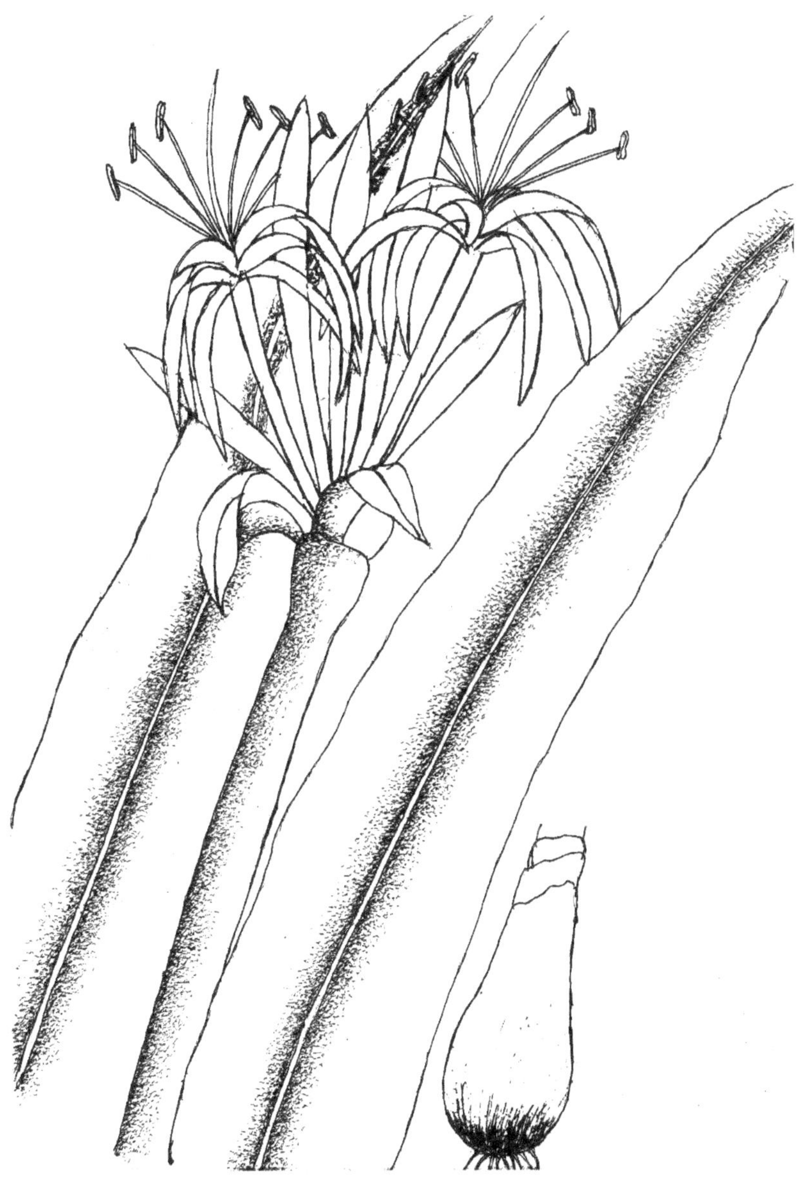

Plate 19　*Crinum latifolium*

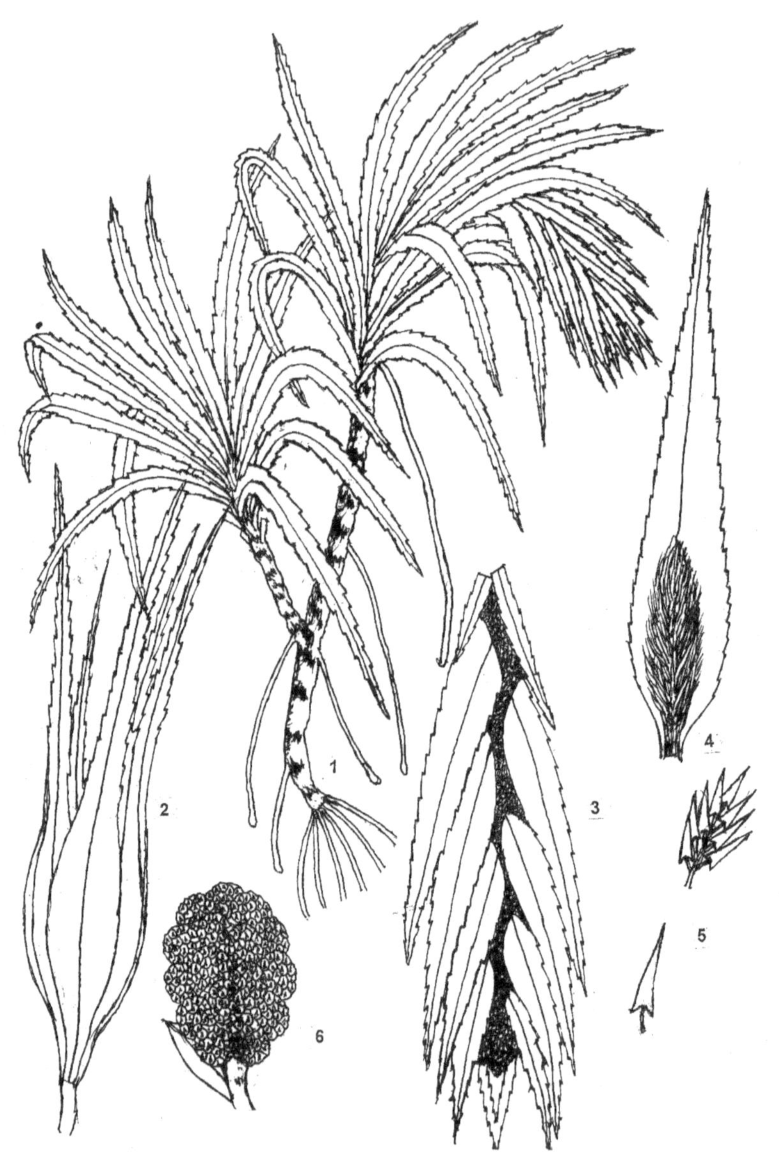

Plate 20 *Pandanus tinctorius;* **Figure** 1 = plant; 2 = Inflorescence, 3 to 5 = Floral parts; 6 = Fruit

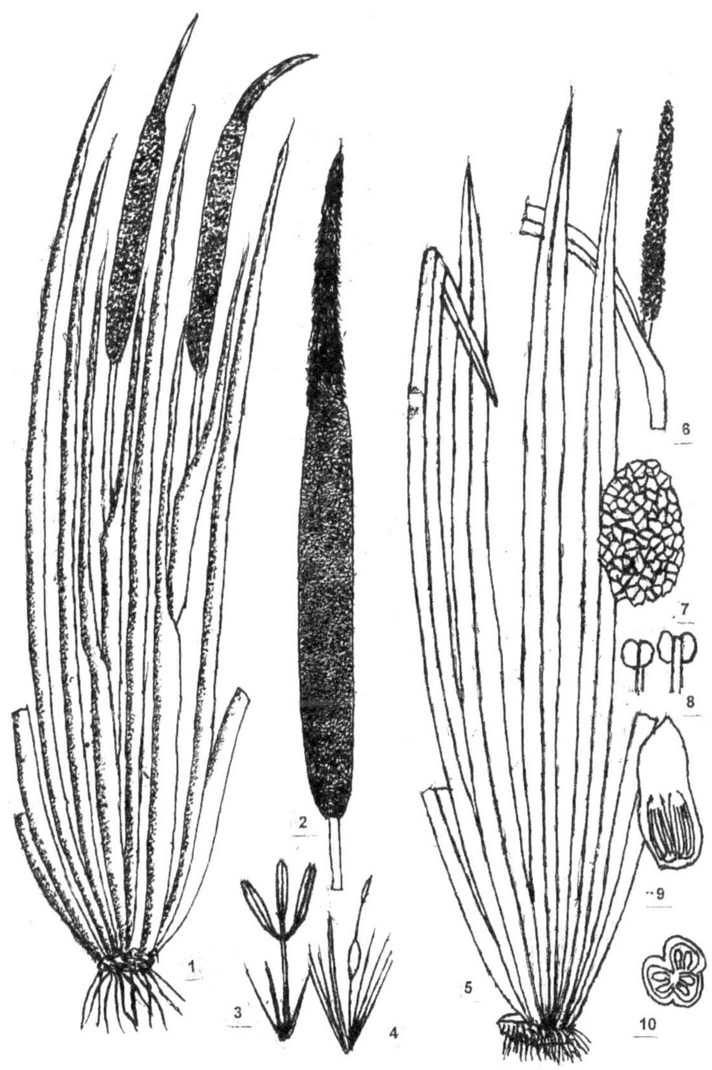

Plate 21   **Figure** 1 to 4 = *Typha angustifolia;* **Figure** 1 = Plant ; 2 = Inflorescens. **Figure** 3 = Male flower; 4 = Female flower; **Figure** 5 to10 = *Acorus calamus;* **Figure** 5 = Plant; 6 = Inflorescens; 7 = Flowers; 8 = |Stamens; 9 and 10 = L.S. and T.S. Ovary

Plate 22 *Cyperus difformis;* **Figure** 1 = Plants: 2 = Spiklets; 3 = A spikelet ; 4 = flower; 5 = Stamens; 6 and 7 = glume.

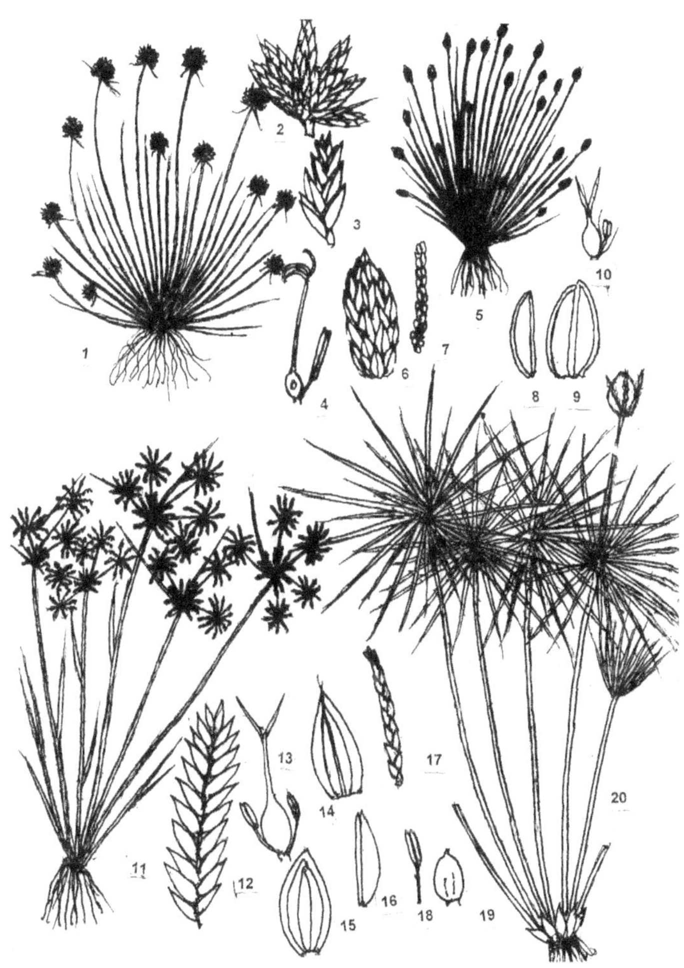

Plate 23 **Figure** 1 to 4 = ***Bulbostylis barbata*** **Athanur form;** **Figure** 1 = plant; 2 and 3 = Spikelets; 4 = Flower. **Figure** 5 to 10 = ***Eleocharis atropurpureus;*** 5 = plant; 6 = spikelet; 7 = Rachilla 8 and 9 = glume; 10 = Flower; **Figure** 11 to 19 = ***Pycreus pumilus*** **Figure** 11 = Plant; 12 = Spikelets; 13 = Flower; 14 to 18 = Floral parts; 19 = A fruit. **Figure** 20 = ***Cyperus rotundata***

Plate 24 **Figure** 1 to 5 = *Eleocharis geniculata;* **Figure** 1 = plant; 2 = spiklets; 3 = Glume; 4 = Flower; 5 = Fruit; **Figure** 6 to 9 = *Cyperus tenuispica;* **Figure** 6 = plant; 7 = Spikelet; 8 = Flower; 9 = Glume

Plate 25 **Figure** 1 to 5 = *Eleocharis dulcis;* **Figure** 1 = plant; 2 = spikelets; 3 = Flower; 4 and 5 = Glumes; **Figure** 6 to 8 = *Cyperus pangorei;* **Figure** 6 = plant; 7 = Spikelet; 8 = Flower.

Plate 26 *Cyperus castaneus;* **Figure** 1 = Plant; 2 and 3 = Spikelets; 4 to 6 = Glumes; 7 = A flower; 8 = Stamen; 9 = nut.

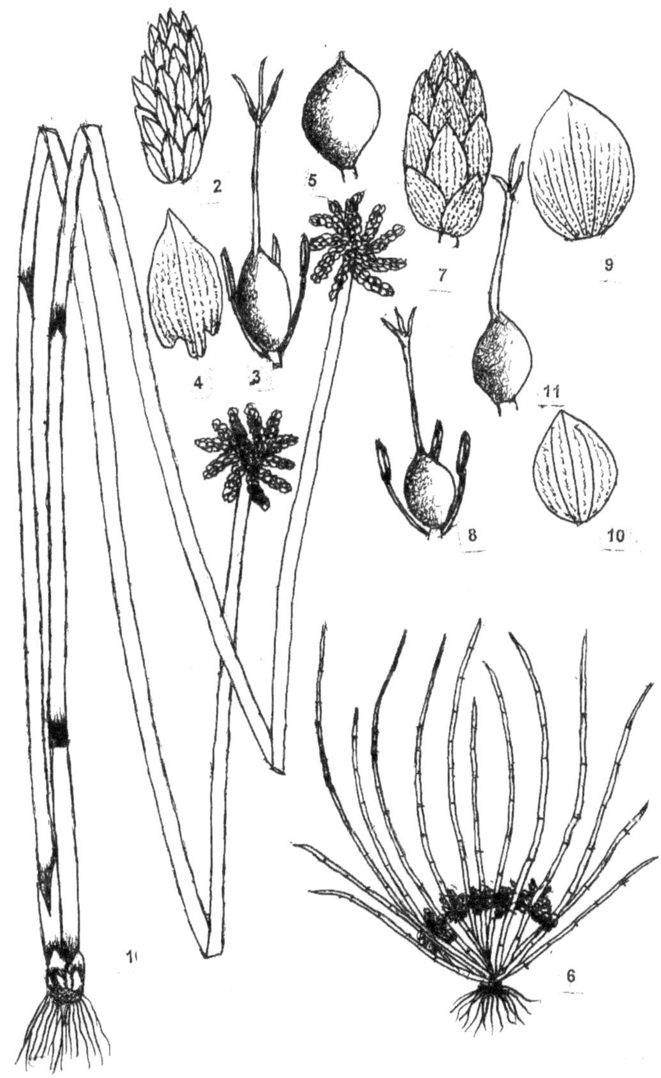

Plate 27 Figure 1 to5 = *Schenoplectus mucronatus;* **Figure**1 = plant; 2 = spikelets; 3 = Flower; 4 = Glume; 5 = seed; **Figure** 6 to 11 = *Schenoplectus senegalensis;* **Figure** 6 = Plant; 7 = spikelets; 8 = Flower; 9 and 10 = Glumes; 11 = ovary.

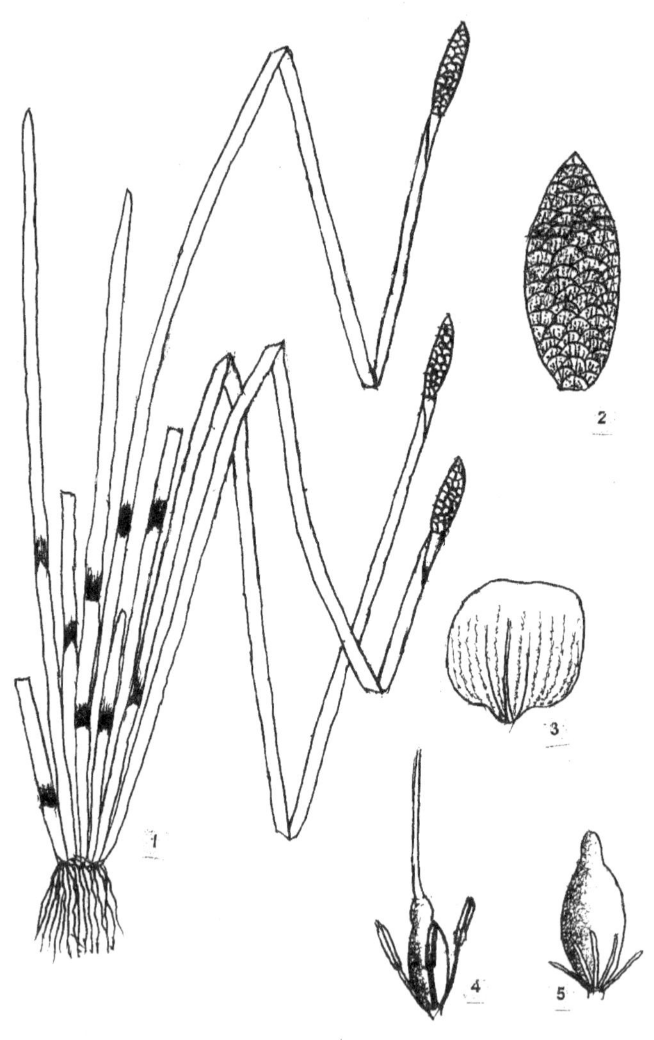

Plate 28 *Eleocharis spiralis;* **Figure** 1 = plant; 2 = spikelets; 3 = Glume; 4 = Flower; 5 = A nut.

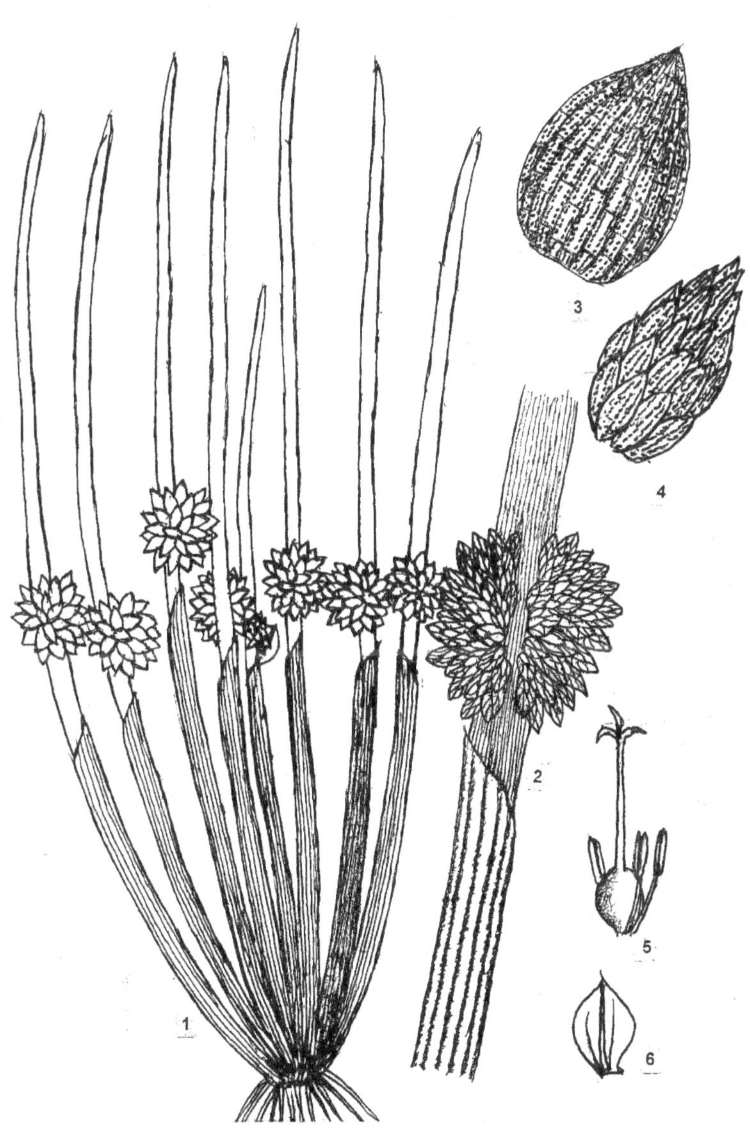

Plate 29 *Schenoplectus articulata*; **Figure** 1 = plant; 2 and 3 = Spikelets; 4 = glume; 5 = Flower, 6 = Nut.

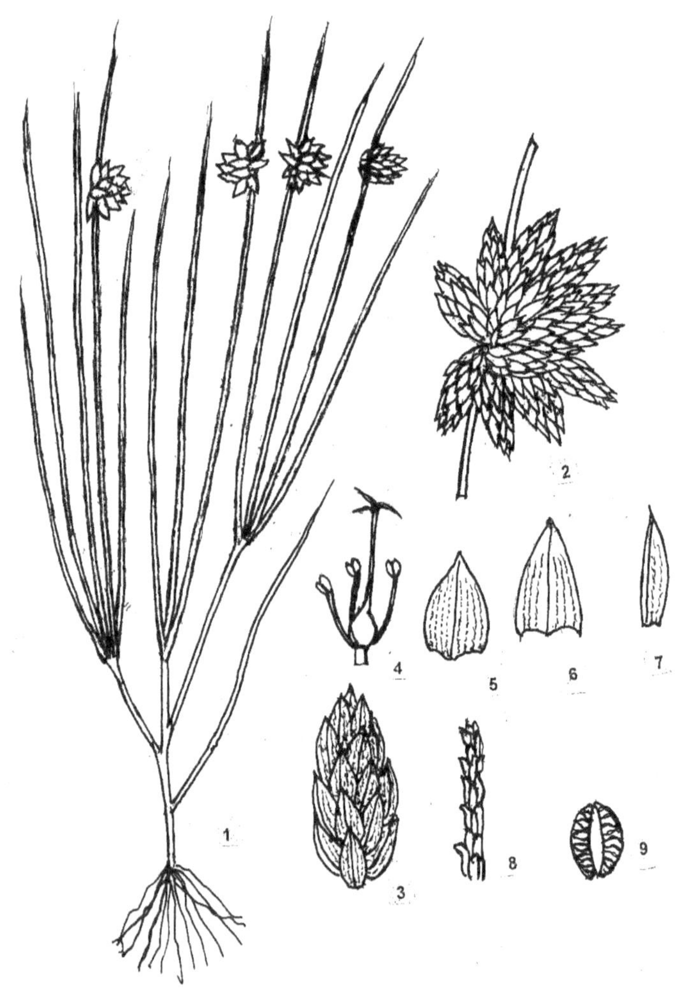

Plate 30 *Schenoplectus lateriflorus*; **Figure** 1 = A plant; 2 and 3 = spikelets, 4 = Flower, 5 to 7 = glumes; 8 = Rachilla; 9 = a nut.

Plate 31 **Figure** 1 = *Cyperus pygmaeus;* 2 = *Cyperus laevigatus;* 3 = *Cyperus triceps;* 4 = *Bulbostylis barbata Chidambaram type*

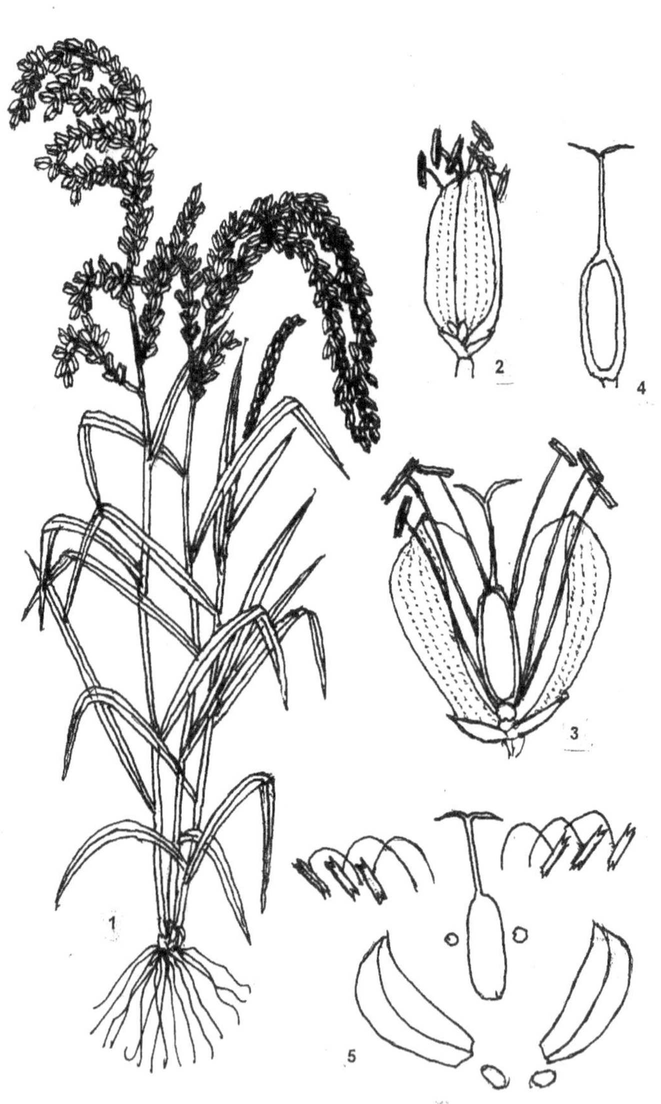

Plate 32 *Oryza sativa;* **Figure** 1 = A plant; 2 = Flower; 3 = flower opened; 4 = Ovary; 5 = Flower ground plan.

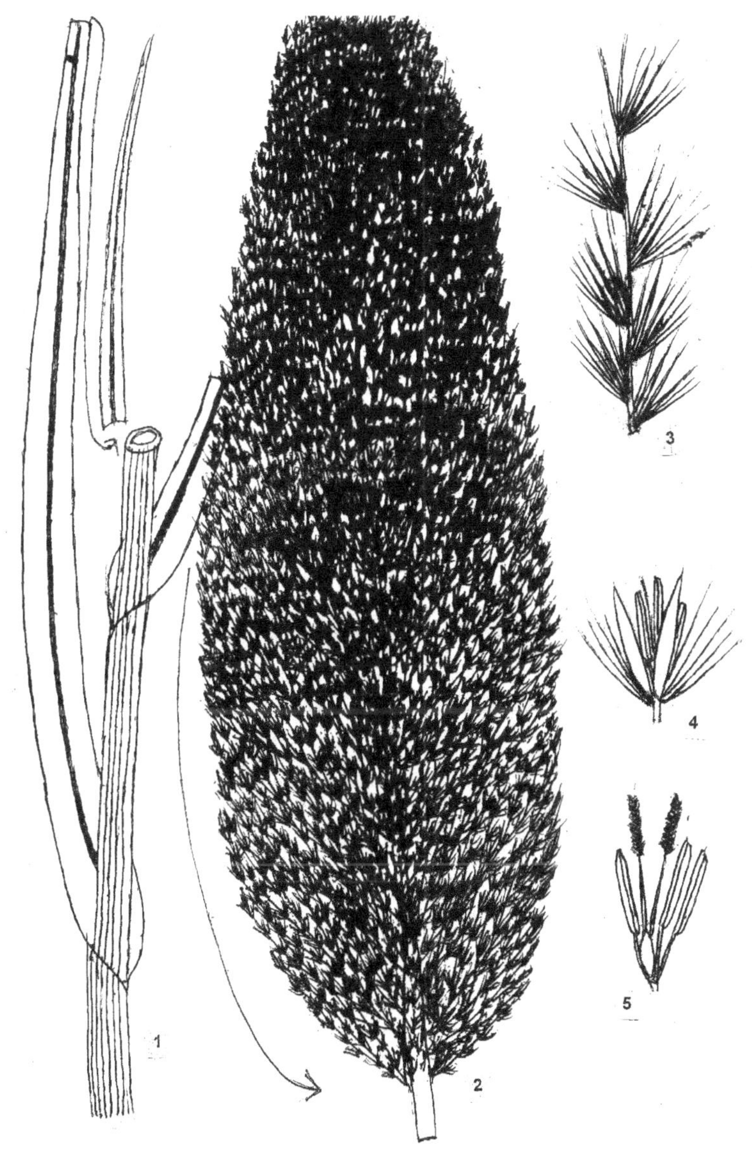

Plate 33 *Saccharum spontaneum;* **Figure** 1 and 2 = Stem and inflorescence; 3 = Spikelets; 4 = A spikelet; 5 = Carpel and Stamens.

CONCLUSION

Hydrophytes and Helophytes are water living and water loving plants. So far, the taxonomists have described the flora of Tamil Nadu in a volume combining the terrestrial plants of the plains and hill stations. Now, the author has tried to describe them into separate volumes as follows, as already stated.

1) Mangrove flora and Marine Angiosperms

2) Hydrophytes and Helophytes of the plains

3) Terrestrial plants of the plains

4) Plants from 1000 feet to 4500 feet elevations in Eastern Ghats

5) Plants from 4500 to 8500 feet elevations in Western Ghats.

Now, it is possible to the author to describe each volume with more informations and in-depth knowledge.

Then and there, the cytogenetical and chemotaxonomical studies by the author and his coworkers have been added in the respective volumes. The ecological adaptations and evolutionary trends of the flowering plants of Tamil nadu have been also added in the respective group of plants.

It is clear that the Mangrove plants and Marine Angiosperms are totally different from terrestrial plants of the plains. Likewise the plants of higher elevations of hill stations like Ooty, Kodaikanal and Valparai are distinct from the plains of Tamil Nadu. Describing all these plants in a single volume will make a total confusion and it is not possible to describe these plants in detail with their adaptive mechanisms and evolutionary trends.

As far as the author is aware, there is no research paper or research book, describing the water loving plants, that is helophytes of flowering plants of India. K. Subramanian (1962) has written a book "Aquatic Angiosperms" describing the hydrophytes of India only. Therefore, describing the water loving plants (amphibious plants) as helopytes is the first attempt of the author. These helophytes are the link or bridge connecting the two ecologically distinct groups Hydrophytes and Terrestrial plants.

REFERENCES

- Fedorou, A.N. A. 1974. **Chromosome number of flowering plans.** Reprint by Ottokoeltz science publishers, n-624, Koenigstein, West Germany.

- Gamble, J.S. (1957) **Flora of the presidency of Madras**, Vol. I, II and III. B.S.I. Publication, Calcutta

- Mathew, K.M. (1988), "Flora of the Tamil Nadu Carnatic, Vol. II. Rabinat Herbarium, Trichy, Tamil Nadu,

- Subramanian, D. (2010) Diversity of Flowering Plants of Kapper Hills of Tamil Nadu", **National Level Seminar on Application of Medicinal Plants and their diversity. Botany dept,** Govt, Arts College, Dharmapuri, Ales No.1.

- Subramanian, D. (2010), "Bio-diversity of Flowering Plants of Adari Forest of Tamil Nadu, **"National Seminar on Recent Trends in Plant Science, Research**." Dept. Botany, Annamalai University, Article 2.52 pp-43-44.

- Subramanian, D. (2010). Biodiversity of Flowering Plants at Karmangudi Forest of Tamil Nadu, **National Seminar on Recent Trends in Plant Science Research. Dept of Botany, Annamalai University, Article 2.54,** p.44.

- Subramanian, D (2011). "Rare and new species of Flowering plants of the plains of Tamil nadu" **UGC National Conference on future perspectives of Botanical Research**. Botany, Dept. Annamalai University, Article NO.114, p.31.

- Subramanian, D (2017). Biodiversity of Flowering Plants as a means of origin and evolution of species" **National Seminar on Recent Advances in plant science Research.** Botany Dept., Annamalai University, Abs No., 10.3.p.74.

- Subramanian, D. (2017) Rare and new flowering plants of Cuddalore District of Tamil Nadu, India. **Plant Archives** , 17(2): 1783-1789.

- Subramanian, D. (2018). The effects of climatic changes on flowering plants of Tamil Nadu. **International conference on Recent Scenerio in plant science Research**. Botany Dept, Annamalai University, Abs. No.1.39, p.24.

- Subramanian, D. (2018) Endangered and Fast disappearing plants of Tamil Nadu due to climatic changes. **International conference on Recent Scenerio in plant Science Research.** Botany Dept. Annamalai University. Abs. no., 1-40, p.25.

- Subramanian, D. 1994. "Proceeding of the National Seminar on "**Cytopolymorphism in Plants**, "Annamalai University Publication, Annamalai nagar, Tamil Nadu.

- Subramanian, D. 1999. "**Cytotaxonomical studies of South Indian Flowering plants**" Manuscripts of the D.Sc thesis awarded to the Author. Annamalai Universiy Publicaiton, Annamalai Nagar, Tamil Nadu.

- Subramanian, D and R.Ponmudi, 1987. "Cytotaxonomical studies of South Indian Scrophulariaceae". **Cytologia. 52:** 529 to 541.

- Subramanian,D 1978. Cytogenetical studies in **Urginea indica (Roxb.) Kunth.** Jour Indian. Bot. Soc. 57(3): 211-218.

- Subramanian, D. 1979. Cytopolymorphism in **Crinum defixum,** ket **Science and Culture 45** : 110-112.

- Subramanian, D. 1971. Cytological investigations in some south Indian Compositae. **Jour. Annamalai Univ. Scince. 29:** 81-87.

- Subramanian, D. 1988. Cytotoxonomical studies in South Indian **Cyperaceae Cytologia** :53: 67-72.

- Subramanian,D. 1991. **Proceedings of the National Seminar on Cytopolymorphism** in Plants, Annamalai University Publication. Annamalai Nagar, India.

- Subramaniam, K. 1962. **Aquatic Angiosperms**, CSIR Publication, New Delhi.

INDEX

L

M

N

www.ingramcontent.com/pod-product-compliance
Lightning Source LLC
Chambersburg PA
CBHW071329130726
47996CB00002B/680